UFOs

OF THE

KICKAPOO

UFOs OF THE KICKAPOO

John H. Sime

atmosphere press

The *UFOs of the Kickapoo* articles originally appeared in the *Epitaph-News* from Viola/LaFarge, WI.

"Wrong Turn into Destiny" originally appeared in the *Epitaph-News*.

"Embalming ET" originally appeared in *American Funeral Director* magazine.

Dedicated to Gary Sime

FOREWORD

by Jay Rath
Author, *The W-Files: True Reports of Unexplained Phenomena in Wisconsin*

In 1896, 50 miles south of Stockton, California, Col. H.G. Shaw was driving a friend in his buggy when they chanced upon a strange metallic craft, 150 feet long and pointed on both ends. Three seven-foot creatures came out and made warbling noises. After unsuccessfully trying to bring Shaw aboard, the visitors and their airship flew away.

In 1955, friends and family near Hopkinsville, Kentucky, engaged in a nighttime gun battle with around a dozen small figures that had emerged from a "spaceship." After four hours they made a mad escape to town and its police station. Local, county state, and military police investigated. They found evidence only of all the damage that had been left by the family's firearms.

In 1957, Antônio Villas Boas, a farmer in Brazil, was taken aboard an egg-shaped craft and experienced sex with a white-haired humanoid with cat eyes. He said.

Or so all of these people said. My first response is disbelief, followed by amusement. I don't need to hear anymore. It's not that their stories are so strange, it's that I'm prejudiced. These people are either: 1) long ago, 2) hillbillies, or worst of all, 3) foreign. They are distant from me in time, experience, and place. They are (ahem) alien to me.

I never mock people who relate these stories, even though I know how to make fun of things. In fact, I'm a professional at it. I served on staff at *The Onion* for a long time, and I wrote for *MAD* magazine. But I've also authored three books dealing in great part with UFOs. I also write for the Britain-based *Fortean Times,* the top journal of anomalous phenomena.

When the term "UFO" was coined, by the Air Force in 1953, it was an attempt to get serious and scientific. Earlier they had been called mystery airships, ghost rockets, and especially "flying saucers," which was intended to describe their motion, not their shapes; they were said to move strangely in the air, defying aerodynamics, as if they were flat stones or—even more smooth—saucers, skipping across the surface of the water.

The new, more scientific "UFO" label caught on, but somewhere along the way, we forgot that it doesn't mean aliens. Nor does it mean, as some have suggested, creatures from inner earth, or secret undersea bases, or time travelers from our own future, or an alternative dimension briefly bubbling into our own, or what they had been called a millennium earlier: signs from God(s).

Forget that and let's start fresh. These are objects that seem to fly, which are unidentified, and a small percentage of the time, remain unidentified after study by military pilots, scientists, radar experts, astronauts, meteorologists, and police. And all those people have seen them, too, along with astronomers.

An astronomer who never did see them, but who studied them most, was Prof. J. Allen Hynek of Northwestern University (1910-1986). Signed on by the Air Force in 1948 to debunk sightings, he gradually was convinced that UFOs were something real, and not visionary or fictitious, which was exactly what some Air Force leaders had concluded, in writing, as early as 1947.

Hynek, being a big-time fancy scientist and everything, invented ways to categorize reports of objects that flew and were unidentified. One way was by the range of proximity. A Close Encounter of the First Kind is of a UFO less than 500 feet away. A Close Encounter of the Second Kind? That's if the object interacts with the environment. It makes your car stall or radio buzz, or your dog barks, or it may even leave landing marks or radiation. A Close Encounter of the Third Kind is when an occupant of the craft is observed.

To Hynek's categories, John Sime now adds Close Encounters of the Kickapoo Kind, and I consider it a refreshing refinement.

Yes, it's easy to laugh off reports from a long-ago California colonel in a buggy, or crab-handed aliens and intergalactic sex, especially if you never bother to read the serious literature. It's much, much harder to laugh when you know the context. A very near neighbor, who lives life much as you do, is difficult to dismiss.

In gathering detailed reports from a relatively small geographic area, John has added communal depth. The result is not a general portrait of alien visitation. It's a portrait of community. Some in this collection of neighbors have secrets to share that may be a little embarrassing or even shocking. It's a tribute to John that they so trust him.

They are too close to us to dismiss. Instead, we must listen, as he does, with the ears of a friend.

WHY UFOS?

Explanatory Note for UFOs of the Kickapoo

Three and a half years after I left the Peace Corps, I saw a UFO and may have encountered some of the occupants. In the case of my experience, I do not use the term abduction, but rather visitation because they came to and entered my house.

There is no doubt about my seeing the craft. It was a classic daylight disc, as they say in the UFO realm, sometimes referred to as Ufology. In March 1982, I was still single and lived alone (except for my black Labrador dog, Jennie) in a small house along U.S. Highway 14 in Readstown, Wisconsin. It was my custom in the afternoon to brew a pot of coffee or tea, sit next to the north-facing window of my kitchen, and listen to my favorite radio program *All Things Considered. All Things Considered* came on at 4:00 pm every weekday. I was in the midst of listening to the show when I noticed something up in the clear, blue sky.

Whatever it was, it was above the hill behind my

house, to the immediate east of Readstown. It was low enough that it was somewhat obscured by the bare branches of the trees. It was early enough in the spring that no leaves had yet appeared. The object at times glinted in a metallic manner through the branches. However, I could not make out a clear shape. There was no doubt that it was moving behind the trees, definitely making progress, albeit slowly, so it was not some kind of kite or balloon caught in the branches of the trees.

However, it was making no noise, so it was not a helicopter, which was the first explanation that occurred to me, since it was moving along so slowly. An airplane could not have moved as slowly as this object. Could it be a blimp? They can move very slowly. Again, there was no noise and I had seen blimps over the years and knew that they were as noisy as helicopters, if not more so.

Well, I thought, why don't I just go outside and try to see it. I quickly exited the back door of the house and my dog followed along behind me. We both walked out into the center of the backyard. By this time the object had moved away from the top of the hill and was now stopped over a house farther up the hillside. To arrive at this location, it had had to move away from the hill and then move downward slightly, maybe one hundred feet. It was not far away from the top of a recently-built, ranch-style one-story house. It was no longer than the house. It was no more than twenty feet above the roof of the house.

The object at the time struck me as having the same shape as a Fisherman's Friend cough drop, a brand of strong menthol-flavored cough drop I frequently took at that time. This means that the top and the bottom were not rounded like a saucer but both were straight. The ends were curved but did not come to a point. The overall effect was not seeing a flying saucer but seeing a flying lozenge. It is interesting that years later, in the early 2000s, the U.S. Navy would take videos of a similarly shaped object off the coast of Mexico which they called "the flying Tic-Tac", after another candy lozenge.

The object I saw in 1982 was made of shiny, silver-colored metal. The surface even glinted somewhat in the sunshine, but not so much that it was hard to look at it. There were no windows, no legs, no antennae.

It still made no noise. My dog paid no attention to it whatsoever and did not seem to be nervous or upset. Instead, she stood next to me, which was common, and did not evince any awareness of anything except my presence. When I finally returned to the house, she readily followed me.

Before I went back into the house, the craft went away most peculiarly. For perhaps a minute or two it remained over the house and then very slowly it moved to the south, toward Highway 14. It remained at the same elevation as the house and went at an extremely slow speed. A walking speed. In this manner, it gradually moved away from the house, from the hill. It took perhaps a minute for it to reach a point directly over Highway 14. At that moment it suddenly shifted its direction of travel to the east, toward Richland Center. It disappeared at the horizon within ten seconds. So, it went from going a few miles an hour, did a 90-degree turn, and suddenly went thousands of miles an hour.

I took no action on what I had seen until the next day when I mentioned it to my next-door neighbor. As soon as I described it to the kindly old fellow, he sensed the out of this world, science fiction elements of my question and immediately laughed and asked if I had seen little green men. I laughingly said no and let the matter drop. I also talked with the wife of the married couple who lived in the house over which the UFO had paused. She did not mention little green men, but it was clear that she thought my question was ridiculous. She chuckled and shook her head as if in disbelief over the fact that I would waste her time on such a ridiculous matter.

So, I never asked anybody else about it. I definitely did not report it to anybody—the military, the police, and authority. I had heard accounts of people harassed and ridiculed after making such reports and after the reaction of my neighbors, I decided that I did not need any of that.

However, for at least a couple of weeks whenever I thought about the event, almost immediately a thought went through my mind which effectively shut down any further consideration: "Whatever it was, it wasn't a UFO." And at that point, I did not think about it again, for a while. And then, when I did think about it again, the same thought again shut down the topic: "Whatever it was, it wasn't a UFO."

Finally, after a couple of weeks, I was sitting in a church on Maiben Street helping with a funeral. I was sitting in a back pew which was next to Maiben Street. The window of the church was colored stain glass, but I was aware of the fact that to the east of Maiben Street was first a line of houses, and then the east ridge (known geographically as Maple Ridge) overlooking the town— the ridge from which the object I had seen in the sky had first come. Once again, I thought of the object, and once again, came the thought: "Whatever it was, it was not a UFO." However, this time there was another thought that came counter to it: "Then what the Hell was it?" And there was no counter thought except the realization that I had indeed seen a craft from another planet, some highly advanced non-human technology. With a sort of shudder, I let the matter drop in my mind and refocused on the funeral.

Two or three weeks after that funeral, I was in my home on Highway 14, sitting in my recliner, watching television. It was early evening, dark, but not yet time for bed. Suddenly, there was a knock at the door. I got up and went to the door. Not expecting any visitors, I was eager to see who could be wanting to see me. It was too late for any vendors or religious advocates. Perhaps some friends were making a surprise visit.

I opened the door and standing before me were two people: a man and a woman. The man was taller than the woman. I have an impression of his being tall and thin. The woman was petite and resembled a woman I had once dated in college. So much so that at first, I thought that is who it was. I greeted her with an immediate and friendly, "Well!" The difference in appearance was that woman had blond hair instead of red hair. In both cases, the hair was parted down the middle and hung down to shoulder length. In both cases, the women wore scholarly, wire-rimmed glasses. The difference in hair color or not, I thought it was the same woman I had known years ago at first, so much so that I was amazed at how unchanged she was despite the passage of almost ten years.

The woman looked at me and said, "The highway is

closed, we have to come in and wait until the highway opens again." Without a moment's hesitation, I opened the door wide and motioned for them to enter my living room. I remember thinking, "Good, I will be able to tell these people about my adventures in Africa and show them some of the things I got in Mali." This was and is one of my favorite pastimes.

At the same moment, as the two people entered, the woman turned to me and communicated not so much with voice as voiceless thought into my mind: "Letting us in is as important as your joining the Peace Corps." I don't recall my dog barking at these strangers or paying any special attention to them.

I have no more memories of the event, nor of the couple after those remarks. I don't remember where they sat in the room, although I did broadly gesture to the couch against the wall. My recliner was at a 90-degree angle to the couch where my visitors usually sat. I don't remember what we said to each other. I don't remember when they left. I don't recall any remarks made by them as to where they came from or where they were going. I don't remember them saying anything about the problem with the highway. I don't remember waking up the next morning thinking about it.

All I recall is that in the coming months and, in fact, years, whenever a thought of the event crossed my mind, I would immediately think: "That was one good thing I did!" And I would feel good about the event and myself. Then I would forget about it, until the next time, when again I would simply think: "That was one good thing I did!" And again, feel good about myself. And then forget it.

Things went on like that for perhaps ten years until one night I was reading in bed. My wife—for by that time I was married—had a job then which often meant that she worked at night. So, I was alone in bed, in our darkened house, reading a book about UFO encounters. I was particularly struck by the unbelievability of some of the accounts. One in particular struck me as unlikely. It involved complete strangers coming to the house of some people who had seen a UFO, asking to come in, and then everything is forgotten about it. This is ridiculous, I thought. Sometimes people have visitors and you forget a few details. Nothing unusual. I had the very same thing happen to me once. And that was one good thing I did.

But for the first time, I began to analyze my memory of the event. Where were these people from? Well, they were... Nothing. Where were they going? Well, they were... Nothing. What did we say to each other? Nothing.

I had to admit that that was strange, but what did other people say? I realized that the next morning I had heard nobody in the village talk about how the highway had been closed. There was nothing on the normally busy gossip grapevine about this unusual event. There was nothing mentioned at the next village board meeting (meetings which I covered as a newspaper reporter). I thought back to similar events that had happened to me or my family when we had traveled. Not once did we leave our automobiles and seek refuge in nearby houses. And what of all the other people in all the other cars that would have had to stop along the highway. Where did they go?

The more I thought about this in the darkness of the night in my bed, the creepier I felt. I vaguely began to feel—well, violated. What had happened? Who were those people? What did we do together? What did they do to me? Why did they come in the door talking about Peace Corps when I had never met them before in my life?

INTRODUCTION TO THE FIRST ARTICLE IN 1991

These are not taped interviews. They are not first-hand accounts; the interviewer rephrased the conversations. But the conversations did take place, and the people who say that they saw these objects do exist. Questions asked by the interviewer are not included in the text, but should be assumed, as the interviewer is not included in the text, but should be assumed, as the interviewer tries to get the witnesses of the UFOs to provide a consistent pattern of information: Place of the incident, approximate date, time of day, activities engaged in prior to the incidents, etc.

Each interview subject featured here, after an initial reluctance, seemed eager to describe their encounter with unexplained craft, and often were willing to draw pictures.

It was originally the plan of the article not to write

the accounts anonymously. But it soon became evident that some people were only willing to tell a highly interesting story if it was to be printed with no names used. Also, since these accounts are not libelous, but perhaps only swamp gas, or Venus, or lost weather balloons, leaving out the names of witnesses does not necessarily compromise the credibility of the article.

Updated Introduction to 2021 Edition

These reports ended up being far more than local stories cadged in cafes, bars, and church dinners. The internet became a source I did not have in 1991. As the years went by, I took stories from various websites but still depicting events in this part of the world. I also began to include UFO-related world and national news, and even obituaries. There are even photos taken in this area.

1991 UFO EVENTS

The Soviet Union under the influence of *Glasnost* releases a significant amount of UFO information.

Wave of UFO sightings in Belgium comes to a halt.

The Space Shuttle Discovery photographs objects flying in space with a flash of light and several objects that appear to be flying in formation.

Timothy Good publishes *Alien Liaison: The Ultimate Secret.*

Local Sightings

A Woman from Viola

This happened in 1972, near Brodhead, Wisconsin. I was ten years old. We lived on a farm near Brodhead. My aunt and I were riding in a car. She was bringing me home from cheerleading class. It was early evening; it was dark out. Suddenly, there was this object buzzing right along behind the bumper of the car. It followed us home. It was in the sky above the car. The camera did not work. We ran into the house, and it zoomed past and hovered over the garage as we watched from the bay window. We watched it from the house for five minutes. It looked like a plate held at hand's length. It was a round object with pulsating lights. When it disappeared, it made a big burst of light, no noise. After she returned to her home it was still visible in the distance.

A Couple from Readstown

It was winter, early evening about 7:30 pm. There were six to eight inches of snow on the ground. This occurred in the middle 1970s. We were getting ready to go snowmobiling. We had on our suits. Right behind the hill, from behind our house, came this object. It was huge, as big as an airplane. It was round and had windows on the bottom side. It moved real slow through our valley (within four miles of Readstown). It made no noise. We cranked up our snowmobiles and headed up the ridge road when it got out of sight. When we got to the top of the ridge, no more than a minute or so by snowmobile, the object was nowhere to be seen. If it had been an airplane, it would have still been visible.

A Woman from Readstown

This took place in 1985. I was going with my brother from Readstown to Viola. It was about midnight. As soon as we got around the corner from Readstown, this thing appeared with red and yellow lights. We thought it was a helicopter or an airplane, but it made no noise. It followed us all the way to Viola. When we slowed down, it slowed down. When we sped up, it sped up. When we got to Kickapoo High School, with its lights, we headed up to it. When we pulled into the school parking lot, the thing still hovered over us. So, we headed into Viola. We went to his house for a while, then it left. I never believed in UFOs before then. Now I do.

A Woman from LaFarge

This happened on our farm, near LaFarge. It was in the spring of 1973. I was outside, and my husband and son were pouring concrete inside a structure. So, they were inside a building across the road from our barn. I was in front of the barn, talking with the tax assessor. I saw this round object which was silver-bluish in color. It was about fifteen feet in across, and ten feet high. It had windows, which were porthole-like windows. There was a front window. It moved over and behind the barn. The tax assessor saw it too. We watched it for almost a minute. We were about fifty feet from it at one point. It glided past our house, then in the wink of an eye, it was gone. When it took off, I heard a little hum, otherwise no noise at all. When I asked the tax assessor what it was, he said he didn't know and didn't want to know. My husband and son did not see it. We called to them, but by the time they got out of the structure to look, it was gone. I don't know if they quite believed us. Since that day, I have talked with other people around here who have seen similar objects.

A Man from Readstown

I was sitting next to a north-facing window, drinking coffee and listening to the radio show "All Things Considered," which at that time came on at 4 pm. So, it was late afternoon. It was spring, 1982. Suddenly out of the north-facing window I saw what I at first thought was an airplane move from behind a hill on the edge of Reads-town. What drew my attention to it was the way it was moving slowly, way too slowly for an airplane to stay in the air without crashing.

I thought maybe it might be a blimp or helicopter, but it wasn't making any noise. So, I thought it might be a glider. I went outside to get a closer look at it. It was still in the sky when I got to the backyard. It was a lozenge-shaped object, longer than it was high, smaller than a house, because by now it has moved away from the hillside and was right over a house farther up the hill from my house, about a block away.

It was a silver-colored object with no windows visible. It moved silently. I watched it from the backyard for about a minute. It moved steadily south at no more than walking speed. When it got out over Highway 14, it made a 90-degree turn and headed east toward Richland Center. It disappeared at the horizon within ten seconds.

A Man from Viroqua

This happened in 1977. It was on a road going down to the Sidie Hollow boat landing. It was in November. It was between 6:30 pm to 6:45 pm. As I came up the road, I saw this object in a field. The object looked like a small Moon, about two or three windmills high. It looked like the Moon had fallen and shrunk. The object was yellow. There were two bright, white lights branching away from the center of the object at the bottom. I saw no windows.

I saw it as I drove up the hill toward the object. It made no noise. There was a small plane flying nearby, and I could see and hear that, but this object made no noise. The object moved slightly, back and forth, left and right in a jerky motion. I did not leave the car. Finally, I reached down for my hunting binoculars and when I looked up again the object was fading away. It faded away as I watched it. I was fairly close to it. It was higher than the trees, higher than two tobacco sheds because there was a tobacco shed nearby. An article was put into the *Broadcaster-Censor* about it. Two people reported seeing it. I've since talked with both of them, and they both saw what I saw, on the same morning. If you plot our three locations that morning on a map, they are in a straight line.

1992 UFO EVENTS

UFOs and the Alien Presence, a documentary film is released by Michael Lindeman. It features Bob Lazar, who worked at Area 51.

In the "Falkirk Triangle" in Scotland, a star-shaped UFO lands on a highway in front of a car, then suddenly shoots off into the sky. Numerous other such reports follow. In August 1992, two ambulance drivers were abducted by ET s who dropped down in front of their vehicle and took them away for examination. They lost an hour of time.

Dr. David Jacobs publishes *The Secret Life: First Hand Accounts of UFO Abductions*. He teaches a UFO course at Temple University.

The International UFO Museum and Research Center in Roswell, New Mexico opens in fall 1992.

Local Sightings:
The Manning/Harrison Hollow Sightings

A Man from Readstown

This took place in the fall of 1969. Haying was done. I was with a bunch of 35 to 40 people at a party on a hilltop hayfield near Harrison Hollow. It was midnight or better. The first thing that we saw was what we at first thought was a star. But it was too bright. It was not moving at all at first, but then it started to come straight down out of the sky like it was suspended on a wire. This lasted a minute or two. It also began to project a sort of beam out of it and down at us. It got closer and closer and the beam covered more and more of the hayfield—which was at least as big as a football field. You couldn't hear a whisper out of this thing. At first, we thought it was some sort of military thing, but it made no noise or vibration. I've seen a few military things since I was in the Marines. We got into our cars and left. The field was still lit up when we left. None of us ever said much about it to anyone, since we were partying and didn't figure that anyone would believe us anyway. But it did happen.

A Woman from Readstown (daughter)

This was in the early 1970s, my husband and I had been somewhere together and came home. It was around 10:00 pm. First, we noticed a really bright light. It was white at first, but it did have some colored lights later. We called over to my mother's house across the valley. We could not get through on the phone at first. When we finally did get through, her voice was distorted and the connection was staticky (even though she is less than a mile away). I'm not sure if I saw it go away, or it went away while I was on the phone.

A Man from Readstown (father)

It was a round-shaped thing. It had bright colors and would move around very fast. It was 1:30 to 2:00 in the morning. It was in the early 1970s. My wife and I had just got home. She called her mother to tell her that it was right over her house. She didn't get through right away, and when she did, her mother sounded like an old, old man.

A Woman from near Readstown (mother).

I remember my daughter mentioning that she saw an object in the sky at the time. I did not see anything. I don't remember any telephone call.

A Man from near Readstown

This was about 1975 or 1976. I was coon hunting with a friend of mine. It was in October. It was around 11:00 pm. We were in Harrison Hollow.

I saw the same thing that I did with my wife, a couple of years back. It made a whirring noise. It was round with different colored lights. My friend never did see it, even though it was right straight above him. It was about 40 or 50 feet across. It was about 500 yards above my friend. At the most, I was about 1/8 of a mile from it. I was on the same level of ground as my friend.

A Man from near Readstown

It was in the fall of 1967. I was all alone in my car coming home from a dance in Viola. I was following a friend of mine who was driving his car just ahead of me. It was about 1:30 am.

We were near the Kickapoo Center bridge. I saw a big ball of light heading through the valley, coming from the Manning direction. It was about hilltop level. It was a big glow in the sky that had several colors. It was oval-shaped. Neither of us stopped. We both sped up our cars and got out of there. When we got to Readstown, we stopped and asked each other what it was. We didn't know what it was, but we both agreed that we saw it.

A Man from Viola

This was in 1967. I saw a bright shining light that had no colors. There was no sound. It definitely was not a satellite.

I was coming home from a dance in Viola. There was somebody behind me, he saw it too. I was going toward Readstown and at Manning, I saw an object that was hovering over a hill to the west. Suddenly, it turned south and began heading in my direction. It followed me to Readstown. If I sped up, it sped up. If I slowed, it slowed. Just at the last curve before town it went up to the hilltop and disappeared.

I don't remember stopping that night to talk about it. I did talk about it at school with my friend in the other car. We both saw it.

A Man from Readstown

Last Fall, my daughters saw something hovering over Nelson's Hill, just north and west of Readstown. It would have been between Readstown and Manning. It was about 10:30 pm. They were on Highway 131, just outside of town, heading south in their car. The object was cigar-shaped, with red, yellow, and green lights. They almost had an accident when they saw it. After a little bit, it shot off into the west.

22

1993 UFO EVENTS

March 31, multiple witnesses across southwest England saw a large triangle-shaped UFO. Some people speculated it was re-entering Russian space junk.

September 26, a large triangle is seen over Bakewell in the Derbyshire Dales of England.

August 10, huge UFO seen over West Point Military Academy in New York is watched by three MPs at 2 am. "This thing was a huge UFO! It looked like a six-story building lying on its side, and it was at least two stories high. It appeared black in the moonlight and was totally silent. It had three huge square lights on the first story, the second story had three square lights on the bottom as well."

Local Sightings: Broader Patterns
Harrison Hollow...LaFarge...The World...

A Woman formerly from the Viola Area

This was in the fall of 1981. I was with some of my friends in a car on the ridge overlooking Manning. It was probably about 8 pm. We were parked in our car, it was a clear night. From the east, in the direction of Viola, we saw an extremely bright star. Within minutes, the hayfield on the other side of the road was lit up. We couldn't find the light source until I stuck my head out the window and looked up. A large craft hovered silently in the sky, lit like a Christmas tree. It was a gigantic triangle the size of a football field. There were bands of light on and some off. They would go on and off in no particular order. It had visible floors that were black metal. It was a windmill height off the ground. It was at least as tall as a football field is long. It was about 50 feet wide.

Our car would not start. There was a beam of light going from the ship to the ground moving across the hayfield heading toward our driver's side. We got really scared, then the beam shut off. Then I felt better and got out of the car. I watched the triangle for at least 10 minutes, standing out of the car.

Then I saw the lights of a farmer's tractor. I ran up to him and he was acting very oddly. He stopped the tractor but did not shut it off. He seemed to be about 60 years of age. He stared straight ahead for a while before looking at me. He had a real blank expression. Finally, he looked at me and said: "What is wrong?" I said: "Look up. Can't you see that?" He looked up and looked back at me and said: "That's an airplane." I looked again, and now most of the lights were off. I walked back to the car. The tractor drove on past our car heading north. A local man who was in the car said he had never seen the man before. We drove around, headed north, and the tractor was nowhere to be seen.

A Couple from Readstown

This was at least 20-some years ago. My wife and I had a cabin in the woods near Harrison Hollow, about ¾ of a mile back from the town road, midway in the woods.

This was a Friday night in the winter. We had come down for the weekend from La Crosse. Our son was coming up from Waterford. He arrived before we did. He, his wife, their three boys, and our younger son were in the car together. They drove halfway up the road and couldn't go any farther because of the heavy snow. They had to walk the rest of the way. Our grandsons went on first. Our older son, his wife, and our younger son, with the family cat in his arms, started out a little later. While our older son his wife, and our younger son walked along the road they could see a light moving along the road ahead of them. Our older son wondered, "Why did those kids take the flashlight?" But the kids did not have the flashlight, as he found out later. The light went away, and when our sons and our daughter-in-law got nearer the house, the cat went berserk and tried to get away. This was odd for the cat, which was usually calm. It made all kinds of scared noises. But our son managed to hang onto it and they reached the house. At the house, they found out that the flashlight was left in the car.

Later that evening, one of our grandsons got on a sled with two milk jugs. He went down to the spring at the foot of the hill to get water. On the way down the hill, there was a light following along behind him. He thought it was someone from the house following him. But nobody had left the house. The next morning, we found no tracks in the snow except our own.

A Couple formerly from La Crosse

My husband and I were at our house on the southeast side of La Crosse, near Highway 33. This was about 25 years ago. It was in the summer and was just getting to be dusk. We had big kitchen windows facing the bluffs to the east. In the sky below the top of the bluffs, I saw something that definitely was not an airplane. It was a hovering disc-like or cigar-like craft that had white lights. I called to my husband (who had knocked his back out) to come and see it, but he did not make it to the window before it disappeared. It shot away to the northwest.

A Woman from Readstown

This was in the late 1970s.

I was driving back from bowling with some of my friends. We were dropping people off in Harrison Hollow and Manning area. The electricity was off all through Harrison Hollow. Several times, always in the northeast, we saw a green, glowing object in the sky that moved a little. It came and went, but was always in the north or northeast. It disappeared before we got to near the Manning Church. The electricity was on at the farms past this point.

A Man formerly from LaFarge

(September 6, 1979) We saw this blinking light in the distance from our house at 11-12 at night. We were all in bed asleep. I don't know what woke us up. It made no noise. I went to get my binoculars, but when I came back, I didn't need them anymore because it was now much closer. It looked as big as a 747. It was probably a couple of miles away. It had red, white, and blue lights that revolved around it. The craft itself was a disc-shaped thing. The lights would constantly change, with the same light turning different colors at different times. After a few minutes it went away.

The next week, two Vernon County Sheriff's deputies and I watched the same thing again for more than an hour. We had to watch it this time with my binoculars because the deputies didn't have any. It zigzagged in the air, making 90 degree turns, doing all kinds of things no airplane could do. The deputies radioed a radar installation in this area, and the radar people simply respond: "Don't worry about it."

1994 UFO EVENTS

The Roswell Incident Recalled: Area 51.

There have been a considerable number of developments on the UFO front in the past year.

The Roswell Incident—the report of an alleged July 1947 UFO crash near Roswell, New Mexico, and the alleged retrieval of a vehicle and alien bodies—has received unprecedented press. Showtime TV cable net-work released a motion picture starring Kyle MacLachlan and Dwight Yoakam. While this was a fictional account, it interwove information, photos, and segments from documenttaries. It presents the whole matter as being a case of a dedicated military intelligence officer (Jesse Marcel, played by MacLachlan) made to lie about a UFO crash by his sinister superiors. Two months after this film appeared, the Air Force released a report on the 1947 incident, which summarized and dismissed

Most of the research done by UFOlogists like Stanton T. Friedman, Kevin Randle, Don Schmidt, and others, and concluded that the whole thing was still a balloon—this time a high-security radiation sniffing device called Project Mogul.

The original government story on the Roswell incident was that it was a weather balloon that had been found by rancher Mac Brazel (played by Yoakam) and that it was fragments of this earthly, mundane item and not mysterious pieces of some extraterrestrial craft brought into Roswell. He took his fragments first to the county sheriff, George Wilcox, who called the military at the nearby Roswell Air Corps base. From then on, it was a government show. All fragments and the rancher were eventually whisked off. The rancher was held incommunicado for a week, and when let loose was reluctant to say nary a word on the subject. The government did not entirely lock up the story, however, not at first. In fact, they initially issued a press release that came right out and said that they had found a "flying disc". This report was released by base relations officer Walter Haut on the orders of Col. Blanchard, base commander. The story was the headline for the July 8, 1947 *Roswell Daily Record*. For a few hours, the story was carried over the wire services, broadcast on the radio, and published in daily newspapers. Reports from around the world, for a few hours, deluged Roswell. Within 24 hours, Army generals had issued the weather balloon report which effectively shut down any press attention.

Although the main thrust of the government's explanation of the Roswell incident is that the whole story was the result of stupidity on the part of Jesse Marcel, the intelligence officer who identified the debris as a UFO, it is interesting to note that this seemingly boob-like error did nothing to Marcel's career. One would normally think that the next assignment of a man who supposedly had caused the government so much embarrassment and wasted time would be conducting the penguin census in Antarctica. Jesse Marcel's next assignment was in Washington with the Strategic Air Command.

In a telephone interview with this reporter on January 28, 1994, Walter Haut stated that there is no doubt in his mind that when Col. Blanchard ordered him to issue that press release that he was convinced that what they had was a craft from another planet.

The recent Air Force debunking attempt was issued partly as a result of actions taken by Congressman Steven Schiff, who represents Roswell in the House of Representatives. He has been pushing on a number of bureaucratic fronts to release any or all documents pertaining to the matter.

The U.S. government has been on the defensive on another UFO front—the so-called Area 51 in Nevada. North by northwest of Las Vegas is an empty desert region known as Groom Lake. It is bordered by Nellis Air Force Base. Groups of UFO activists have taken to traveling to the edge of this area and confronting the camouflage-wearing private security personnel. It is the belief of some of these people that captured UFOs are tested here. It is definitely known that top secret testing of the Stealth airplane and the U2 was done here. Stories have also circulated in the Las Vegas area for years concerning a secret base there behind the mountains where up to 1,200 people work every day after being flown in on jets. Robert Lazar, a physicist, has maintained on camera that he researched an intact extraterrestrial vehicle housed at Groom Lake.

Rachel, Nevada has become a sort of haven for this

type of thing as it is the closest settlement to the desolate Area 51. A computer wiz, Glen Campbell of Boston, has moved in recent months to Rachel and set up shop as proprietor of the Area 51 Research Center. He produces a monthly computer magazine on CompuServe called the Groom Lake Desert Rat. A couple of weeks ago, Larry King hosted a live TV call-in show on the Turner Network called UFO Live. Campbell was a guest, as were Stanton T. Friedman and Kevin Randall, who talked about the Roswell story.

The internet has proven itself to be a great boon to the field of UFO research, as now people can talk directly to each other, from around the world. In a sense, this eliminates the media middle man. Everyone can become his own news magazine.

Also in 1994, Professor John Mack produces *Abductions*, a study of alien abductions using hypnosis. Mack was a Harvard professor and a winner of the Pulitzer Prize in 1977 for his biography of T.E. Lawrence (aka Lawrence of Arabia).

Local Sightings

A Woman from Soldiers Grove

This happened in the fall, sometime in the middle 1980s. It was 3:00 pm or so. I was on Halverson Ridge, in my car with two other people—relatives from out of state. We were just driving around. We were headed north. We came over a rise. We stopped when we saw this bright light north and west. It was high in the air. We stopped and sat there and watched it. It did not move fast. It disappeared so fast you could not tell where it went to. The sun was behind and west of us. Even an eye doctor's exam light would not be as bright as this was. After it disappeared, we met a township worker who said he also saw it. He said that until we appeared, it was headed toward him. He said he had been scared.

A Man from Soldiers Grove

This happened on Halverson Ridge, between the Kroning farms. It was in the broad daylight. It was a ball of light in the sky. For a while, I watched it in my township truck as it bounced back and forth in the sky. Then it was headed straight for me, going in no other direction except toward me. It was not a weather balloon because it was not following any air stream. That's what attracted my attention because it was doing turns that no airplane could do. It came right at me until another car showed up. Then it went backward just as fast. It took off ten times faster than any jet. My hair stood straight as a string.

A Man from Readstown

A friend of mine and I had just finished working in a hayfield about sundown. It was summer. It was 1991 or 1992. We were on a farm east of Viola.

We were sitting on a round bail and we both saw an object that was perfectly round in shape. In comparison to the sun, it was the size of a dime held out straight. It was a deep, bright, red color, and was as bright as the sun. The sun was already set, however. This was twilight. The sun was gone. We had suddenly noticed this round object in the sky in front of us. We were facing south. The object just seemed to appear, it did not come from any particular direction. When we noticed it we both noticed it. It shot off to the right (which would be to the west), and we both observed this. Then it shot off to the right again and disappeared. We both watched it for at least a minute and talked about it later after we had seen it. Neither of us could come up with any solution unless it was some kind of secret government craft or something from another planet. When it moved, it went fast and appeared to shimmer or shake.

Quote from *Above Top Secret* (Page 303) by Timothy Good, that relates to the three above sightings:

"During a talk given to the Tulsa, Oklahoma Astronomy in 1982, former Air Force intelligence officer Steve Lewis revealed that the twelve years he spent investigating UFOs for the military both in the US and abroad convinced him that intelligent extraterrestrial beings are visiting Earth. Apologizing for being unable to be more specific owing to strict orders from the Air Force not to divulge specific details about his UFO research from 1965 to 1977 (including a period with Project Blue Book), Lewis stated that only a fraction of the information accumulated by the military has been released. He admitted that although the majority of sightings have a mundane explanation, the bona fide reports are often associated with a common feature of very bright, blinding lights. The Air Force believes that the light may be related to an advanced propulsion system, enabling UFOs to travel at the speed of light, Lewis said."

A Woman from Readstown
It was my daughter-in-law's birthday, August 1, 1976,

that's how I remember the date. It was about 6:00 pm. and I was sitting at the dining table in my daughter's house in Onalaska. Their backyard was clearly visible through her sliding glass door. Behind their backyard is a small rise with some trees. My daughter had left the room when I noticed something hovering above the trees behind the house. It was not a saucer-shaped thing. It was taller and was brightly lit. There were two things on the bottom that looked like wheels. I was about 75 feet away from it. It made no noise. Then I stood up and called to my daughter. Just as soon as it moved it disappeared, just like it had heard me. When my daughter came it was gone.

A Woman from Switzerland (via email)

This took place in Langenthal, Switzerland on Thursday, June 7, 1994, at 9:30 pm. It was a "Close Encounter of the First Kind" (the sighting of craft with no interaction with occupants). From the bottom, it looked like a triangle, from the side it had a small "dome". In color it was dark gray or black. The side sort of glimmered. It was about ten meters long. From the ground it was between 50 or 100 meters. It moved vertically for about ten minutes and then disappeared. It was a beautiful summer night with no wind, no clouds.

This note is added by our computer correspondent: "Here in Switzerland it is a problem to find some stories about UFOs. A few months ago, some people saw a UFO over a highway, but no newspaper has printed the story. Not one!"

At least they can't say that about the *Epitaph-News*.

1995 UFO EVENTS

The most dramatic UFO-related news of this year concerned the telecast of a film of an alleged autopsy of an alleged dead alien allegedly recovered in 1947 in Roswell, New Mexico. The film was shown on the Fox Network on August 29. Many observers pronounced the film a fraud.

A number of criticisms have been leveled against the film. The owner of the film refuses to permit the destruction of even one frame of the film in order to perform chemical tests that could determine the age. Critics have also pointed out the fact that the camera seems to shake or go out of focus whenever a closeup of the alleged internal organs is attempted. The nature of the contamination suits worn by the operators, the existence of a coiled wall phone cord (in 1947), and the fact that blood readily flows from incisions made on camera (not likely to happen in post mortem situations) have all been pointed out.

Special effects experts from Hollywood have been quoted as saying both that the film is too real not to be true, and that the film would not be hard for a competent special effects artist to manufacture.

Another UFO-related news story concerned the investigation conducted by Harvard University into one of its psychiatry professors—-Dr. John Mack. Mack, a winner of the Pulitzer Prize, began interviewing people who allege that they have been abducted by ETs. He produced in 1994 a book called *Abductions*, which attempted to examine the phenomenon largely from a psychiatric perspective. He also appeared as a speaker at a number of UFO-related conventions.

Harvard University responded with an investigation of Mack and his methods. For a time, it seemed likely that he would be dismissed from this Ivy League institution. However, in the end, he was let off with a warning.

A member of Congress, Rep. Steven Schiff, of New Mexico (who represents Roswell), requested a Government Accounting Office investigation of the alleged UFO crash in Roswell. The result was inconclusive as that agency discovered that most of the records for that base in 1947 had been destroyed. This might sound like a "smoking gun" of evidence destruction; however, it was also discovered that records of that time for other bases were also destroyed, perhaps for reasons of storage.

Jack Anderson, an investigative columnist, took a look at Roswell at the time of the GAO investigation. "But we do believe something did happen at Roswell," said one source close to the investigation. "Something big. We don't know if it was a plane that crashed with a nuclear device on it....or if it was some other experimental situation. But everything we've seen so far points to an attempt on the part of the Air Force to lead anybody that looks at this down another track."

Also in 1995…1961 UFO abductee Betty Hill produces her book *A Common Sense Guide to UFOs.*

Local Sightings

A Man from Readstown

I think it was in 1989. It was February, it was Wednesday during Lent, it was just after Lenten Services at Peace Lutheran in Readstown. It was about 9:00 pm. or 10:00 pm.

I was in my bedroom, which faces west. Suddenly, I noticed a very bright light hovering over Nelson's Hill (ed. This is the ridge west of the Kickapoo River in Readstown). The light was very large, although not as large as the Moon. The center was very bright. It was not perfectly round, it just radiated light on the outer edge. It wasn't very far off the hill. It made no noise. It almost looked like a helicopter looking for something, but it made no noise. There was no searchlight coming from it.

My mother was in the next room, so I called her to look at it. In the time it took her to come, it started to shrink. We both saw it shrink down to a red, low, pulsating light. It got dimmer. Almost as if it went away to the west. This was not like a blinking airplane light. It was much slower. Sometimes it would go completely out.

When it was bright, it did not move. But when it was red and pulsating it started to move along Nelson's Hill to the north, then out across the valley, around behind the village to near the school. It took about five minutes to make this trip. After it was behind the school, it went off to the east over the hill. The whole time it was treetop level. We probably watched it altogether for 10 to 15 minutes.

A Woman from Readstown

It was on February 15, 1989. It was a Wednesday after Lenten Services. I tried to keep a mental note in case I ever crossed paths with anyone who saw anything like it.

It was about 10 minutes after 9:00 pm. We had just gotten home. I was playing the piano in the recreation room and my son was upstairs in his room. He shouted for me to come and look at what he saw in the sky.

The first that I saw it, I was in the living room looking to the west where my son now was. It almost looked like it was on top of Nelson's Hill, just sitting there. It was definitely low to the hill. I didn't see any shape, just a very bright white light.

Then it took off suddenly, going very high in the air, heading up to the northeast. I can't really describe how it left. It shot off into the distance and appeared to turn into a reddish, pulsating light. It was not an airplane. In fact, there was an airplane that went directly over our heads going on an east to west path. The thing we were watching was north of that.

The airplane was very visible. There seems to be a flight path in that direction. The airplane did have blinking, red lights and it was different than the pulsating, glowing, red look of the other object. It was much farther away than the plane.

It didn't make any sound. We stood outside on the

balcony watching it. We did hear the airplane. At the time, I called the policeman's wife and by the time he was available, there was nothing to see. Nobody else seemed to see it. I don't think we watched for as long as 5 minutes.

A Man from Viroqua

I was 12 years old when this happened in 1968. It was a hot summer night; my cousins were visiting and we were camping outside on our farm on a ridge south of Viroqua. It was about 1:00 am or 1:30 am. We were talking and watching the sky for stars and airplanes. South of us, we noticed a small, but fast-moving light low in the sky over a small valley. It got down below the tree level in the valley and we didn't see it again. We at first thought it was a helicopter, but it was moving too fast.

That's all we saw, but we learned that at about the same time a neighbor boy, who lived on the farm on the other side of the small valley was coming home. He saw the same light in the valley and his view was not obscured by trees as was ours. He became curious enough that he went out behind their farm buildings to get a closer look at it. What he saw out in their field was a circular thing, about 20 feet wide, with lights running around it. He watched it raise off the ground and take off. He didn't recall any noise.

The LaFarge Ghost Light

Several reports have surfaced over the months concerning a mysterious light seen over the years in Lawrence Hollow, north of LaFarge. The most dramatic account came from some coon hunters, who were hunting there one night a few years ago in the fall of the year. These men were carrying lights with them and so when they noticed a light on the other side of the valley, they at first thought other hunters were in the area. However, this light began to move through the air, along the hillside in a manner impossible for a walker to duplicate. The witnesses fled the scene and report the impression that "there is something up there".

Explanations for this phenomenon range from the folkloric to the scientific. One account attributes the light to the ghost of a young boy sent off for the cows. The boy never returned. The fate of the cows is unknown. From the scientific realm comes the explanation that the light is actually caused by the fumes of petroleum long felt to exist in the northern Kickapoo Valley (hence the name of the settlement "Oil City").

The fall of the year is usually regarded as the most likely time for the light to appear.

Tips for UFO Watchers

Arnie Nelson, an astronomer and a science teacher at Wausau West High School, was interviewed in August 1995, by the *Wausau Daily Herald*. He provided the following hints for people who think they see UFOs.

- Relative brightness—How bright is the object compared to the stars, distant lights, of the Moon. Does it cast a shadow?
- Relative position—If you put a fist at arm's length, how many fists high would it be (this is a 10-degree measure)? How did it move among the stars? Time the object's motion. What direction did you first and last see it?

- Conditions—Were you in a car or looking through a window? Exactly where were you when you saw it? What time was it?
- Confirmation of sighting—-Ask another person to look, but don't suggest what to look for. Also, try to photograph.

(Thanks to Richard Heiden of Milwaukee)

1996 UFO EVENTS

UFOs entered the public consciousness in 1996 to an unprecedented extent. Several motion pictures and television shows utilizing a UFO theme appeared, including *Independence Day*, which became one of the top grossing films of the year. *X Files* continued to gain popularity, and new shows such a *Millennium* and *Dark Skies* joined the UFO wave.

Moreover, NASA announced studies on a meteor fragment from Mars which could be the first scientific proof of life outside the planet Earth. The first planets outside our solar system were also identified by astronomers.

Perhaps the most significant UFO-related development was the "release" of the Rockefeller Report. It is titled *Unidentified Flying Objects Briefing Document* and is subtitled "The Best Available Evidence." Laurence Rockefeller, 85-year-old financier brother of late Vice President Nelson Rockefeller, commissioned the 169-page report on the "best available evidence" on UFOs, his personal interest. Rockefeller has given financial support to such

UFO researchers as Dr. John Mack and Dr. Steven Greer. He has also urged President Clinton to release information on UFOs both through the White House Science Adviser, John Gibbons, and personally when the Clintons vacationed last year at Rockefeller's ranch in Jackson Hole, Wyoming. This report was not for press release and the 1,000 privately printed copies were given only to high-ranking political and military leaders worldwide.

The report was written by Don Berliner of the Fund for UFO Research, with assistance from Antonio Hunees and Marie Galbraith. Rumors of this report have percolated through the UFO community for months, however, to date nobody has yet broken the code of silence by releasing it to the general public.

Close Encounters of the 4th kind, that is to say, "abductions" or "contacts," were not addressed in this report. This continues to be the single most controversial aspect of UFOlogy, and any report of such should be subjected to the most rigorous analysis possible (see sighting 7B1).

Two large crop circles appeared during the Summer in England. Crop circles have long been linked to UFO sightings. At 6:30 am, farmer Arthur Carrington discovered in East Field at Alton Barnes a formation that was 648-feet long and which had 89 circles that form two strands of 77 circles winding around 12 circles in a line. Because of the similarity of the shape to DNA strands, this crop circle is called the "Double Helix of DNA Strand crop circle". The "Julia Set" crop circle appeared on July 8, south of Stonehenge. It is a 915-foot spiral in a wheat field made up of 149 circles.

Budd Hopkins published *Witnessed*, an account of an

alleged UFO abductee who was taken by ETs within sight of Brooklyn Bridge in New York. The female abductee was levitated through the wall of an apartment house to a waiting craft. People who witnessed it thought it was a movie being filmed. Among the witnesses was a major United Nations diplomat.

Local Sightings

A Woman formerly from LaFarge

I used to live near Valley. It must have been in the early 1950s. My husband and I were coming home up on Morning Star Ridge. As we got nearer to our place, we saw these lights and my husband said it looks like it's in the oats field and as we got closer it was. The road has been changed since then. There used to be two houses— one small one near the curve in the road as you go downhill and the oats field was behind it. As we got closer it absolutely amazed us. I am very naïve and too dumb to be afraid, but my husband was a very timid man and wouldn't stop as I asked him to (he is now dead).

He said: "We will go home and go up on our ridge and see if we can see them". This was impossible. It was too far away and there were too many trees. He did drive on the ridge and, of course, we couldn't see the other place.

The lights looked like landing lights—they never moved. But they were over three stories tall. After all the years, my husband and I disagreed on only one thing. I thought there were wire posts from there to the ground and he thought some plane or something in the air let down the lights. They were in rows like radio towers I've seen when I travel near towns and big cities. Only they were so bright they lit up the woods until I could see the ferns and berry briars. There were three rows and as we drove closer the bottom lights nearer the ground were coming on dimly to bright. Our oat field was long and narrow with woods and trees nearby on either side. There were more woods as we went down the hill and more open on the side of the road.

The next day I called up a neighbor and talked with his wife and asked her if she saw the lights and she said, "Yes, but I thought they were hunters".

But something funny was going on. One of her sisters came to see her on the Wednesday before the Sunday when we saw the lights. She wasn't at home, but her sister told her that all the way out the ridge she saw a helicopter and a police car patrolling the road. It was the following Sunday, about 9:00 pm to 10:00 pm. when we saw the lights

We were very close to the lights and saw nothing else although the entire area was lit up very brightly.

A Person from LaFarge

About a year ago, I was returning from a visit to the Wonder Cave grotto in Rudolph, and I was driving home later at night on Highway 131 between Ontario and LaFarge. Along the government land about a mile south of the big bridge, my truck just died—the whole electrical system went out. I was about to get out of the cab and look under the hood when this bright light just sort of hit me. It's kind of hard to describe, just a kind of ozone smell in the air, then a huge overwhelming flash.

I must have passed out because the next thing I knew

I was laying on some kind of table. I tried to move but my arms and legs were strapped down. As I looked around, I saw I was in a metallic chamber of some kind. The walls were kind of a dull stainless-steel color. There were no instruments, dials, flashing lights, or anything, just these blank metal walls.

Then I heard some kind of voices and these beings were all standing around the table. They were somewhat humanoid in shape and they were all female. Their eyes glowed with a deep red light and their skin was shiny and metallic—some silver, some gold, and copper-colored. The metallic skin seemed alive and pliable, kind of like those space blankets or some other insulating material.

The women began to examine me with some kind of probe device. I was in total terror by this point and tried to struggle but then the probe emitted this purple gas and I slipped back into a dreamy state. I think the aliens took samples of my bodily fluids while I was in this state. When I came back to consciousness there was only one alien standing over me. She began to speak, in a midwestern accent but sort of artificial sounding, like through a synthesizer. She told me that her people were watching us and they just wanted to examine me, then I would be returned unharmed. I was not supposed to talk about this with anyone. Then she sprayed more purple gas from the probe and I passed out again.

The next thing I knew I was back in the cab of my truck. My radio was blasting and all the lights and flashers were on. After I turned everything off, I kept hearing these owls hooting and I even saw some owls sitting in a nearby tree. The ozone smell was still in the air. I started up my truck and got out of there as fast as I could.

I never told anybody about my abduction and I tried to forget it ever happened. I still feel kind of weird though, and I think the alien woman put some kind of implants in my body. I am still afraid to drive that road and I go out of my way to avoid that stretch of highway at night.

Commentary

The first letter is an actual memory of an unexplained or unexplainable event, while the second letter, in my opinion, is an imaginative work of fiction.

The second letter deserves some attention. The light in the sky motif ("huge overwhelming flash") is similar to the movie *Fire in the Sky*. The ozone smell in the air, as well as the strapping down of the arms and legs of the abductee also seem to come from this film. Most believable abduction accounts indicate that the ETs do not bother with straps or other restraints as the abductees are somehow made paralyzed.

Whitley Strieber's book, *Communion*, is also probably a source of inspiration for this letter. Compare this passage from the letter: "She began to speak, in a midwestern accent but sort of artificial sounding, like through a synthesizer" with this passage from page 19 of *Communion*: "The voice was remarkable...It had a subtly electronic tone to it, the accents flat and startlingly Midwestern." A striking similarity to say the least!

There are other similarities. In both the letter and in *Communion*, the examining ET is female. In both cases, the abductee is probed. In the letter "bodily fluids" are removed (an echo of Sterling Hayden in *Dr. Strangelove?*), in *Communion*, fecal matter is removed. Then there are the owls. From the letter: "After I turned everything off I kept hearing these owls hooting and I even saw some owls sitting in a nearby tree." From page 21 of *Communion*: "I awoke the morning of the twenty-seventh very much as usual, but grappling with a distinct sense of unease and a very improbably but intense memory of seeing a barn owl staring at me through the window during the night." From Strieber in *Communion*, the owls become a sort of screen memory of the abduction. The author of the letter is clearly not attempting to block memory of the "abduction".

As for the female ETs in their shiny, metallic, silver, gold, and copper-colored skin, it is hard to decide whether the inspiration is a recent Madonna video or the robots on *Mystery Science Theatre 3000*. Perhaps both.

1997 UFO EVENTS

1997 was the 50th anniversary of what has come to be called "The Roswell Incident". The one, definite, undeniable fact of the whole matter is that a U.S. Army press relations officer issued a release which came right out and said that a flying saucer (or disc) had crashed in the desert outside of Roswell, New Mexico. For the record, here is the text of that press release:

"The many rumors regarding the flying discs became a reality yesterday when the intelligence office of the 509th Bomb Group of the Eighth Air Force, Roswell Army Air Field, was fortunate enough to gain possession of a disc through the cooperation of one of the local ranchers and the Sheriff's office of Chaves County. The flying object landed on a ranch near Roswell sometime last week. Not having phone facilities, the rancher stored the disc until such time as he was able to contact the Sheriff's office, who in turn notified Major Jesse A. Marcel of the 509th Bomb Group Intelligence office. Action was immediately taken and the disc was picked up at the rancher's home. It was inspected at the Roswell Army Air Field and subsequently loaned by Major Marcel to higher head-quarters."

No, there is nothing here about alien bodies. Moreover, even this press release was retracted within 24 hours and replaced by the famous weather balloon story. In fact, the Pentagon still sticks to the balloon story, although it has been updated into a super-secret Russian A-bomb sniffing Project Mogul balloon. Just this spring, the Defense Department held a press conference where they released a study reaffirming the Project Mogul theory and adding a new element—the repeated stories of alien bodies are the result of small test dummies released on balloons in the 1950s.

There is no point in rehashing all of the Roswell pros and cons. Suffice it to say that July of 1997 saw almost 100,000 people come to Roswell, New Mexico to commemorate these events, real or imagined. Events ranged from the scholarly to the absurd. Scientists who have made careful metallurgical studies of alleged UFO fragments rubbed shoulders weirdos who believe they are the Royal Viceroys of the Planet Mongo. The whole phenomenon was symbolic of the entire subject of Ufology, with all of its fascinations and madness.

The locus of activity in Roswell was the now famous International UFO Museum and Research Center. This reporter did not attend the July events but did visit the museum in September when the crowds and the desert heat had diminished. This facility is housed in a former movie theater along Main Street in downtown Roswell. One of the members of the board of directors is Walter Haut, an art gallery owner, longtime Roswell resident, and incidentally the press relations officer who issued the above press release. This reporter has spoken on the phone with Haut many times and is convinced that he was not part of a blizzard of stupidity to sweep Roswell in the Summer of 1947. Something happened, what we may never know in our lifetimes.

This anniversary was perhaps the stimulus for the publication of a number of important UFO books. The most talked about was *The Day After Roswell* by former Lt. Col. Phillip Corso of the U.S. Air Force. If this book is to be believed, the history of the past fifty years will have to be completely rewritten. In short, Corso, who was once a military aide in the White House under President Eisenhower, alleges that the UFO crash in Roswell was real and that much military technology introduced since World War II has come from back engineering of the wreckage—specifically the Stealth airplanes, night vision goggles, computer chips, fiber optics, and so on. This list is astounding. Either the man is the greatest tale teller since the days of Paul Bunyan, Pecos Bill, and Mike Fink or he has written the real history of the second half of the 20th century.

Another important book was *Witnessed* by Budd Hopkins. In short, this book makes the astounding claim that a woman was abducted by a UFO in 1990 in downtown Manhattan in plain view of the Secretary-General of the United Nations and his bodyguards. There are many more aspects to this story too complex to be explained here, but anyone with even a casual interest in the UFO subject should read the book and make up his or her mind.

Cosmic Voyage by Courtney Brown (an associate professor of political science at Emory University) is an example of the envelope being pushed a bit. In short, this book alleges that alien civilizations have and still continue to live on Earth. Some individuals took these theories and connected them to the Hale-Bopp Comet of earlier this year and concluded that...well, who knows what they concluded. But the result was the Heaven's Gate mass suicide of spring, 1997. This event should serve to be a wake up call for UFOlogy. If we are going to be interested in this type of study, we must not play games with peoples' lives.

The most important sightings of 1997 took place in Phoenix, Arizona. A triangular object over one mile in width was spotted by dozens, even hundreds of people over that city and other parts of Arizona. Much media attention was given to it. The descriptions of it are similar to objects seen in recent years over the Hudson Valley of New York State and over Belgium. A number of crop circles appeared, including several in the Wiltshire area of England which tends to be the part of the world most frequently visited by these formations. One crop circle that was 400 feet wide was found across the highway from the Prehistoric ruin of Stonehenge. One formation allegedly appeared before the very eyes of a nearby camper who reported orange balls hovering over the field as shapes appeared on a wheat field.

On August 13, 1997, a crop circle was reported near Wausau, Wisconsin. Photos of this were taken by the *Wausau Daily Herald* and have already joined the worldwide assortment of crop circles on the internet.

UFO abductees have long talked about implants put into them by alien visitors. In 1997, Roger Leir and Darrel Sims announced the results of the investigations of alien implants. They have removed and analyzed items taken from the bodies of abductees described as implants. The results of the analyses indicate that the objects contain out of Earth elements.

Local Sightings

A Woman from the Coulee Region
Yes, I am what you would call a "contactee". You may well ask, what does an experience with aliens and/or UFOs feel like? I have had hundreds of experiences that bend the borders of the known, earthly reality.

And yet, I am puzzled as to which would be labeled as extraterrestrial phenomena. In my youth, I was having out-of-body experiences and assumed I was dealing with discarnate entities or spirits. In my later years, I came to realize that many of these episodes dealt with aliens. What I have learned is that those we might feel comfortable calling "spirits" are also "aliens" and vice versa. This is especially true when we learn that spirits and most aliens are from various dimensions. I exclude the technically superior, but spiritually empty "Grays" from this category though. I believe they're primarily three-dimensional and are made up of organic compounds like us. They may appear interdimensional, however, because they can go in and out of our time like most aliens can. Only they can't do it naturally. They can only do it with mechanics.

Another incident you would no doubt label "alien" was on a night in Sept. 1990, when a human-looking woman appeared a few feet from my bed. She was wearing a silver suit with a tight-fitting hood. I was fully awake and watched her for a couple of minutes, noting she was only visible from the waist up. I was totally comfortable about what was happening as if I maybe knew her from before. Seconds after she vanished, I felt something placed over my knees. I looked down but couldn't see anything. Then quite suddenly I became very relaxed and just drifted off to sleep.

No, I've never seen a UFO, but have seen black, unmarked helicopters on four or five occasions. They flew very low over a remote canyon I once lived in.

Other than the direct experiences I have mentioned, there are what I call not so coincidental encounters where you learn or share information.

I knew a rancher in New Mexico who had photos of crop circles back in 1984. An accidental meeting? I think not.

I have also traveled to Alamogordo, NM in the spring of '85 to meet with a friend of Swiss farmer, Billy Meier. Meier had close encounters with the Pleiadeans since his youth and had the world's most extensive film and photo collection of actual UFOs. It was at that time that I learned lessons of discernment. A lot of crap gets mixed in with the truth. I believe that Meier's story was legitimate. Unfortunately, the group that formed around him had devolved over the years into a cult. Meier was not to blame. Both his children and he had had many threats on their lives. So, the pressure on him was enormous. He had also suffered a severe head injury which might have scrambled his mind a bit.

In any case, this personal investigation of mine led me to getting a phone call from Phoenix from Lee Elders, a former industrial investigator turned UFO sleuth.

Although years later he was maligned, I believe he had proven Meier's story was true. Elders told me that Col. Wendell Stevens, who helped him investigate the Meier case, had been falsely charged with raping a minor. Apparently, the girl changed the story three times in order to find a time that the Colonel was actually in the U.S.A. during the alleged rape. Although I knew private investigators and UFO witnesses were often humiliated and ostracized publicly, it illustrated to me that dealing with the authorities was truly the dark side of the UFO phenomenon.

I've also been guided to meet one of the best-known abductees, Betty Andreasson, (known now as Betty Luca) who has also been hounded by the authorities via wiretaps and low flying helicopters and has even had her life threatened.

I've also had a "chance" meeting with an itinerant miner who has been given specimens from the Roswell UFO, right before it crashed. Something shot out from this famous UFO as it raced across the sky and landed in a state other than New Mexico. Residents, who prefer to remain anonymous, said they couldn't touch the site for three days because the ground was so hot. What I held in my hand were heavy, pale green specimens dotted with holes like Swiss cheese, as if the substance had once been molten. I believe it was an amalgamation of whatever landed, mixed with rocks and earth. The curious thing was that some of these cut specimens had metallic spheres inside them. The miner had them tested by NASA labs and they reported that these "rocks" were neither meteors nor tektites and that the particular spherical formations could have only been formed in zero gravity.

Also imagine my delight when I discovered that a sibling of mine, who works for the intelligence community, had once been shown material from the Roswell crash that has been used in the Stealth Bomber. Our time for talking openly with one another hasn't arrived yet, due to the secrecy of their job, but the time will come when we are both ready. Coincidence?

I was once asked by a child what planet I was from? If I focus on this lifetime now I can only say, I am from Earth, which includes past lives if seen within linear time. And yet I have had a couple of adventures that tell me that it is also possible to be living an entirely different life on another planet and/or vibration—simultaneously.

Once others begin to live inside the skins of their other multidimensional selves, they will expand their notions of reality. It has always been a part of the divine plan for volunteers, like ourselves, to spiral into the densest vibration and fall into the illusion of separation, and forgetfulness of who and what we are, where we came from, and why. But it is also a part of the divine design, and our destiny, for all of us to return to the light, spiral back to the prime creator so we can say, "Hey, I may sometimes appear as a mere spark of God, but you are and I am you. We are one." The prime creator experiences different planes, different vibrations by splitting off from itself in order to experience itself as other. It's a grand experiment that I am grateful to be a part of.

A Man formerly from Readstown

It was in the early 1970s. It was fall. It was about midnight. We were traveling on Highway 56 going toward

Viola. We were just beginning to climb up Liberty Hill.

The thing we saw appeared to have the outer shape of a blimp or saucer. It was the height of a blimp but moved way too fast to be a blimp. The bottom portion was lit up with orange-colored light. When it disappeared it headed toward Viroqua.

A Woman from Romance

It was a balmy October night, very similar to the weather we have been enjoying recently that mimics late summer/early fall. It was a Tuesday and it was also Halloween night. It was about 7:00 pm. and I had just finished work in Viola. I headed west on Highway 56 toward home which is in Romance. I traveled from Viola to Viroqua without event following my usual routine of going slow until I reach Sheldon's Junkyard for fear of hitting deer on the move. I reached Viroqua, made one stop (hoping Halloween merchandise was already half price, to my disappointment it wasn't), and was on my way again heading west on Highway 56. I must have traveled about three or four miles when I noticed a bright object in the right-hand corner of my windshield. It was bright white (naturally) but it also had a pale blue light that did not burn as steady as the white did. Yet it did not blink. It waved in and out. I guess you might say it pulsated. I watched this thing while I was driving trying to figure out what it was. At first, I thought it was a bright star putting on a spectacular show because it visits Earth at this time of the year and at this time of the day. Then I thought no, this can't be a star because it seems to be moving or staying with me as I traveled the curves of Highway 56. I figured it must be a plane. Yes, it must be a plane. But as I got closer to my turn off point, and after watching this bright object follow every twist of Highway 56 and never leave the right-hand corner of my windshield, I found myself doubting that this was an airplane.

I was soon to end my travel on Highway 56. In about three miles I would turn off on another road. I started wondering whether this strange night-time object would follow me all the way home. I got less than two miles before my turn off point, which would begin my descent into a valley, watching my traveling companion follow me all the way. And as I anticipated turning, this bright object took off like a shot from a high-powered rifle and disappeared over the horizon. As I drove down into the valley, I kept searching the sky for this strange bright white object, but it was no longer visible to me. It disappeared as quickly as it appeared. And even today I still wonder what I saw on that clear Halloween night.

A Man from Readstown

It was in 1952. I was at a dance in Readstown. It was in the middle of the summer, maybe July. Me and a bunch of other guys noticed colored lights dancing over Nelson's Hill, a hill west of Readstown village. They were not stars and not airplanes. They were different colors. Then it shot off north at amazing speed. I stood there trying to figure out what I had seen. After a minute I took off and went to the game. I haven't told a soul since this happened because I was afraid that no one would believe me. But, trust me, the truth is out there.

A Man from Readstown

This was in July of 1997. We were in Readstown from

9:30 pm to 10:00 pm. near the fire station. We looked up at Nelson's Hill. We saw lights moving in all different directions. They were orange, yellow, and other colors. They would move really slow at first, then move fast, then they would stop.

We watched them for a couple of hours. Then they disappeared. At one time there were five or six of them. We saw this on other nights for about a week. Other people saw them too. We haven't seen them since this summer.

The Mystery Airship of 1896-97

The coverage of the 50th anniversary of the Roswell Incident has provoked recall of what might have been the first UFO visitation in the U.S.A. It also might have been the most spectacular journalistic hoax of all times.

On November 17 of 1896, reports began to appear in American newspapers of a strange airship seen in the sky. Many reports described only a light in the sky. Some reports described a dark "cigar shape" in the sky. A streetcar motorman said he saw "a flying machine propelled by two men working bicycle pedals". These reports first appeared in the *Sacramento Bee* and the *San Francisco Call*. On Nov. 25, 1896, reports of this craft were received from eleven different places in California, including Auburn, Chico, Fresno, Hayward, Napa, Oakland, Pasadena, Petaluma, Sacramento, San Lorenzo, and Visalia.

Spring of 1897 saw numerous appearances of this craft in the Midwest. The first appearance of the craft in the spring of 1897 was in Kansas on March 26. There was a dramatic report of a crash of the airborne vehicle with a windmill in Aurora, Texas on April 19, 1897 (*Dallas*

Morning News) which took the life of an occupant of the vehicle (whose body was allegedly buried in the local Masonic Cemetery).

Illinois was the center of activity of the alleged airship in the spring of 1897. Numerous sightings were reported (including in Chicago). Two messages were allegedly dropped from the airship to the ground—one in Astoria, Illinois, and one in eastern Wisconsin. The Illinois message was supposedly addressed to Thomas Edison, who allegedly read the coded message and pronounced it: "pure fake".

After the Midwest sightings, the airship seemed to vanish.

What was this thing? The general opinion is that it was a "vigorous journalistic hoax". While there were primitive dirigibles in existence at the time ("La France" and "Luftschiff") none of them could have managed to travel more than a few miles at a time in still air. None could have traveled from California to the Midwest over the Rocky Mountains under any circumstances. This would not be accomplished for more than twenty years after 1896-97.

It has been pointed out that more established newspapers, such as the Chicago *Tribune* and the San Francisco *Chronicle*, tended to give less attention to the reports than less influential papers. There was also a practice among big city newspapers of the time to print fake items as a joke and watch them spread throughout the small-town papers throughout the nation.

1998 UFO EVENTS

Art Bell Quits

Art Bell, syndicated radio talk show host of the "Coast to Coast" and "Dreamland" shows heard by 19,000.000 people on over 400 stations, announced live on the air at the end of his Oct. 12, 1998 show that he was leaving broadcasting.

His popular show is a mixture of UFOs/conspiracy theory/new age topics. His rich, baritone voice slides easily from describing new UFO sightings to peddling prostate cures. He is a friend to long-haul truck drivers everywhere. His show is also on the cutting edge of computer technology by making his shows available on recorded computer audio.

The website http://www.artbell.com still functions and contains UFO photos and web links to previous guests.

Bell cited a "family threat" as the reason for his departure and refused to elaborate at the time, although he promised an explanation in the future. Bell had on previous broadcasts made guarded references to a threat to his family. Rumors flooded the internet within hours—a government-run conspiracy to silence this man who knew too much, a threat made by one fanatic (with anthrax topping the list of possible methods), a stunt coolly calculated to boost ratings, a corporate dispute involving the syndication company have all been put forth as explanations.

Since quitting, Bell has received more attention from the mainstream press than ever. Until now, he was largely a cult figure who might be mentioned in an occasional reference on *X-Files* or *Saturday Night Live.*

Last week, on Bell's show (now hosted by a guest host), Bell announced that he will be returning to the air on Wednesday, Oct. 28. Internet rumors have continued to churn—now alleging that there is some kind of legal problem involving one of Bell's children.

Stanford UFO Conference

Laurance Rockefeller has long used his great wealth to fund UFO research. Last year saw the release of *Unidentified Flying Objects Briefing Document—The Best Available Evidence,* copies of which were sent to every government on the planet. He funded this report. This spring, he funded a conference on UFOs at Stanford University in California. Seven reputable scientific researchers on the subject presented their best available evidence to a scientific review panel. The UFOlogists involved were Dr. Illobrand von Ludwiger of Germany, Dr. Mark Rodeghier of Chicago, John F. Schuessler of Houston, Dr. Erling P. Strand of Norway, Dr. Michael D. Swords of Eastern Michigan University, Dr. Jacques F. Vallee of San Francisco, and Jean-Jacques Velasco of

Toulouse, France.

The review panel concluded that UFOs deserved serious research by government and academic experts. The topic of alleged alien abduction was not discussed by the final report.

UFO Hotspots

Mexico City continued to lead the world as a scene for UFO sightings. Large scale, massive sightings seen by thousands of people have been a common event in that city and other Mexican cities since July 11, 1991. On that day, there was a solar eclipse which was filmed and photographed by thousands of people. However, in addition to the eclipse, these same people saw and filmed numerous UFOs. Jaime Maussen, Mexico's most famous TV reporter, began broadcasting these reports which continue to the present day.

Washington State was the scene for literally hundreds of reports of green lights in the sky since this summer. One observer reported that he studied one of these lights with a high-powered telescope and that it resembled a meteor or other rock-like item. However, it moved back and forth, up and down, and at times came to a complete halt in the sky.

Local Sightings

A Man from West Lima

This was summer 1969. It was about 7:30 in the evening. It was before dark. My older sister, my grandpa, and I were in the chicken coop. I heard my mother and father yelling: "Oh my God! Look at this!" there was fear in their voices—fear, shock, awe, all wrapped into one. And then the three of us ran out of the coop to see what was going on. It was maybe 500 to 300 feet away from us. It was huge, maybe 150 feet long. It was oval but segmented. It was so illuminated, there were like lights and things. It was very colorful. It moved very slowly. It was just maybe a meter above the tassels on the corn. As it went, the tassels broke on the corn, there was not any wind, but the tassels just broke clean. There was a constant hum. Then we all kind of got ourselves together. Nobody said anything because we were just awestruck. There were about eight of us there. I wanted to run down there and touch it or at least get closer. It was going so slowly that you could have just run down there and hopped on it. We watched it for at least twenty minutes. It was almost like it was examining the crops. Because when it crossed the road, kind of like a steer that knows the fence is down will hesitate on going over to the other side. But it did cross the road. On the other side of the road, we had melons and it seemed to be examining them. It kept going straight heading north toward the city of Watertown. Years later (10 to 15 years later), I learned that other farmers on the path north from our farm did see it. I've talked to at least three other families that saw it that same day. My father told us all in our family to say nothing about it. I also learned that other families decided not to say anything themselves. The closest family to us was milking and the old man, their son, and the old lady all saw it. They never said anything to anybody either. They said that people would have thought they were nuts. That's what Dad said to us too.

A Follow-up from the Mother of the Above Witness

Talk about something like this and people think you're nuts.

Your sister came up to the house. Talk to her. She remembers a lot more. We didn't really pay any attention at first. Just kid stuff. Grandpa came in and said: "You've got to see this."

All of us went out. I'm thinking, well, it's just a semi-truck or something. But there was no road. This thing was just moving across the field. And there really was no sound, which struck me as odd. There were lots of lights. Red and white. Red lights on top. Just below the white lights rotated. They didn't flash, they rotated.

There was no discernible shape that I saw. Just lights. You and your sister might have seen a shape. It was still light when you saw it.

I'm not saying what I saw. I mean the government does all sorts of stuff. I can't say for sure what I saw. I pass. People saw it. I mean I saw lights in houses going out to the north as it moved on. Obviously, they were looking at something. Hey, this guy isn't going to mention us by name, is he?

I don't want people to think we're nuts. But I did see something.

A Man from Viroqua

It was July 30, 1998, between 1:00 am and 2:30 am. Two of us saw it—myself and a friend. How it started out was we were down in the valley watching a meteor shower. Every now and then we heard and felt a bass-like sound.

We got back up to our house on the ridge and we saw

what looked like a giant runway on the horizon in the direction of Cashton. It was a long line of runway-like lights, then we noticed just appearing in the sky over the runway were small lights that rose into the air and came back down, always to the right. They would go to the right, straight down, then to the right again, and finally disappear next to the runway. We watched for 45 minutes. We watched 15 or 16 of these lights go up and come down. Sometimes they went up in groups of 3 or 2.

We finally went to bed and the runway lights were still on.

The next day I drove out in that direction and found no airport or landing strip or anything else that could have been an explanation.

A Man from Desoto

It was 1971, I was living in Melrose. I was driving at night on Hwy 54 toward Black River Falls and I saw what I at first presumed to be a tail light of another car. As we went up the highway, the highway made a curve to the left. However, the presumed tail light went to the right and crossed a cornfield. Then it rose into the air as it approached some trees. I even stopped the car and examined the cornfield for tracks—there were none.

Internet Sightings

(These two sightings from the internet—National UFO Reporting Center (NUFORC) website)

Occurred: 9/9/1998 01:25 (Entered as 09/09/98 0125)
Reported: 09/25/1998 10:27
Posted: 09/26/1998

Location: Tomah, Wisconsin
Shape: Cylinder

Looking east, saw what appeared to be a meteorite traveling north to south. Looking up at about 45 deg. And following the object for about 60 deg. Left to right for about 15 sec. Object was about the size of half a dollar at arm's length. It was white/blue with a small trail behind it. The object had a glow around it. It flashed out, then appeared following the same path as the large object was on. They were bright white and lasted for about 2 sec. more, then disappeared completely. The night was very clear, very little pollution. I think this was Space Junk, I have seen a lot of meteorites and a few pieces of junk reentering before, I do know what aircraft look like and what they can and can not do. This is why I believe it was Space Junk.

Occurred: 9/25/1998 00:40 (entered as 09/25/98 00:40)
Reported 9/25/1998 19:24
Posted 9/26/1998 Location: 80 miles NW of Milwaukee, 6,000 ft. MSL, WI
Shape: Oval

I'm a cargo pilot who flies a nightly run between MKE (Milwaukee) and EAU (Eau Claire). At 0040 central time, My co-pilot and I witnessed a very intense light, so bright it was a light blue in color move from directly overhead our aircraft northbound over the northern horizon. There was absolutely no tail associated with this craft. In addition, the size was that of a pea. It traveled slightly slower than the speed of a meteor but faster than a satellite. The two of us observed the object. It was so bright you could see it pass in front of a vivid northern light display.

1999 UFO EVENTS

Art Bell Events

This was not a year of new discoveries on other planets, it was a year of lawsuits and courtroom discoveries. Last year's departure of Art Bell from the radio airwaves for about one month had ended in a legal battle. Bell, who left radio abruptly on October 13, 1998, in a brief cryptic announcement at the end of one of his call-in shows, was found to be acting to protect the life and safety of his teenage son, who was at that point victim of a child molesting, AIDS-infected high school teacher. A lawsuit was pending against the teacher and the school district and criminal charges were pending against the teacher. It was to concentrate on his son fully and to avoid a possible suicide attempt by the boy that Bell left the air briefly last year.

For a time, after he left the air on October 28, 1998, Bell did not speak about these reasons, since the matter was still in court. Finally, the time came when the molester of his son was found guilty and sent to prison, where he now is. Nevertheless, in that intervening period, rumors swept the internet and the talk radio world as to the real nature of Bell's problem. WWCR, a shortwave radio station in Nashville, Tennessee, had a talk show host named Ted Gunderson (a former FBI agent who has written about an alleged government conspiracy in the Oklahoma City bombing) which featured a guest who flatly stated that the reason Art Bell left the air was that he, Bell, was charged with child molesting. Robert A.M. Stevens is a Missoula, Montana computer expert who put this rumor out on his website. David Oates, an advocate of the New Age pseudo-science of playing tape recordings backward to get hidden messages, was also involved in this. As a result, the radio station, Gunderson, Stevens, and Oates have all been hit with lawsuits by Bell. It is still in litigation.

UFO Lawsuits

Meanwhile, in Phoenix, Arizona, Peter Gersten, director of the Committee Against UFO Secrecy has gone to Federal Court to sue the truth on UFOs out of the government and anybody else he can find. He is also suing two long-time UFO researchers, Peter Davenport and Dr. Steven Greer, both of whom maintain that government officials have told them that UFOs are real. If this is true, then these men should be made to reveal the names because these government officials are in essence breaking the law. This case will hit the courts sometime in December.

Dr. Steven Greer is the founder and director of the Center for the Study of Extraterrestrial Intelligence (cseti.org). Greer holds somewhat controversial seminars in which participants attempt to communicate with UFOs using flashing lights, beacons, and even remote viewing (or ESP). It is the later technique that has led some people to label Greer a huckster or even a cultist. Nevertheless, in his book "Extraterrestrial Contact", published this year, he states that in 1993 he briefed James Woolsey, the then Director of the Central Intelligence Agency, on the UFO phenomenon. Woolsey has since published a letter stating that the meeting was more along the lines of a dinner party, but the two men did meet.

Mars Over Miami

Mars was in the Space news this year when on Sept. 23, the $125 million Mars Climate Orbiter broke apart or burned up while approaching the Red Planet. The orbiter was designed to study the atmosphere of Mars and look for signs of water. This is not the first spacecraft to run afoul of Mars. Conspiracy buffs on the Internet were quick to poohpooh NASA's explanation of a scrambling of English vs. Metric measurements.

Among those insisting that NASA was not telling the truth was former NASA scientist Richard C. Hoagland. He has made a career out of promoting his theory of a "Face on Mars" which he asserts is a ruined intelligently built monument.

Hoagland achieved an Earthly success this year by saving a Pre-Columbian ruin from the bulldozers in downtown Miami. The circle was discovered last Fall during the demolition of a series of 1950s era apartment buildings on the Miami waterfront. To quote the website (at http://savethecircle.org):

"The Miami Circle is characterized primarily by a series of 24 main basin rectangles which have been cut almost 2 feet into the site's oolitic limestone bedrock, 6 smaller ones, and hundreds of random 'post holes'. the 30 large and small 'rectangular basins' form a ring geometry approximately 37 feet in diameter, with approximately 500 smaller round holes scattered randomly across the entire circle's width, if not beyond..."

Mainstream archeologists have concluded that the site was the work of the Tequesta Indians who lived in the Miami area from about 2,000 BC to the time of Spanish colonization. Hoagland and others lean toward the theory that the structure might be the work of Atlantis or ETs or both. But nevertheless, despite Hoagland's offbeat theories, it is undeniable that he was the Man of the Hour this spring when he saved this archeological site from destruction. He mobilized his supporters on his website (enterprisemission.com) and on the Art Bell show and website (artbell.com) to send letters, telegrams, emails, and faxes to the Governor of Florida and the Mayor of Miami. They did. The result was the site has been declared a protected site.

This success was nearly brought to a tragic end later in the summer when Hoagland suffered a heart attack and nearly died in a Miami hospital. After bypass surgery, he is recovering, but at a less frantic pace than before.

UFO Sightings: Two Men from Readstown see the same thing

A Man from Readstown #1

It was in January or February of this year. We left Readstown about 6:40 am. heading to work in Viroqua. We saw it at the approximate location of the ceramic lawn ornament shop (editor's note: just past the wayside at the intersection of County J and Highway 14). My friend was driving. He told me he had just seen a bright star-like object move through the sky and stop. I looked at the object and it did look like it was twirling or doing something different, then all of a sudden it went off like a light. Kind of as a joke, I said to my friend: "Flash your lights at it." Then it came back on! But as a smaller light, which was now red and blue and was also moving about in a sort of pattern. As we drove up Highway 14, it was mostly on the left and moved gradually to the right. We saw it for the next two days. The second day it kind of moved more than the first time.

A Man from Readstown #2

We saw it between the Highway 14 wayside and the ceramic shop, it was about a quarter to seven. I think it was in January of this year. I was gazing at the stars to the west or left of the road. I said to my friend in the car with me: "Look at that falling star. It's just sitting there." And when I looked back it was still just sitting there. Then it faded in and out and in and out and then went out completely. Then I flashed my headlights at it and then it reappeared again. But this time the lights were like twinkling. Like a beacon on a school bus. It was like a perfectly round object. I would say it was six to twelve inches in circumference and about 2,000 feet in the air. Then after a bit, it shot off, straight up but in an easterly direction.

I saw it the next day too, and I also flashed my lights at it, and it shot off in an easterly direction and disappeared.

Alien Visitation?

It was a beautiful day in Southwest Wisconsin. I had taken the whole summer off and had not done any physical activity since the prior autumn. My husband and I were out in the woods getting a good start on our winter supply of wood. We worked hard all day Saturday and did not notice anything peculiar other than the unusually good weather. In hindsight, that in itself was ominous. We hauled four pick-up loads of split firewood to the house.

That night we relaxed with a few beers, still noting the unusual weather. The so-called "Milky-Way" was floating overhead, appearing closer than normal. This made me apprehensive, so I had another beer. After going to bed, I noted a slight buzz but soon fell into a heavy dreamless sleep.

Sometime in the night, I was transported from my bed and alien physicians removed all the muscles from my body for some reason they took samples of my muscles, thus shortening them considerably. With surgical skills unmatched in our world, they replaced the shortened muscles, leaving no scars, no sign of blood, and no indication that I had been removed from my husband's side. They removed all memory of this procedure from my consciousness. The only sign that I had been thus violated was my inability to walk in an upright position the next morning, or to do otherwise heretofore simple acts such as reach, stretch, bend, or twist.

A Woman formerly from Soldiers Grove

My husband and I were at a campground north of Phoenix, Arizona. It was about 11 pm. and my husband

and I were on a mesa observing the sky. Suddenly, we saw a small car accident down below on the highway. Just a minute later, we noticed an object which reminded me of a railroad train in the sky—a black object, dotted with something like windows or a string of lights. The object came from behind a mountain in the same direction as the car accident. My husband, who had been in the Air Force, said to me: "That thing is going to vanish all of a sudden and we are never going to see it again." We watched it hover in the air for about five minutes. Sure enough, it suddenly took off and flew away almost instantly. A couple of years ago we were watching a show on television about the lights over Phoenix, Arizona. When we saw that we knew that it was the same thing that we saw.

2000 UFO EVENTS

UFO Files Sold

The leading topic discussed in the field of UFOlogy throughout the year 2000 was not crashes or sightings, but ethics.

For years, abductees have been interviewed and videotaped by a variety of abduction researchers. Some of these researchers have presented themselves as therapists—either helping those traumatized by abduction or those who through mental illness have deluded themselves into believing they are abducted. Now, a scandal has developed within the UFO field in which some of these abductee files have been sold.

Much of the controversy surrounds the organization called MUFON (Mutual UFO Network) and a man named Robert Bigelow, a Las Vegas real estate billionaire who has long donated research funds to such UFO researchers as Budd Hopkins, David Jacobs, and Linda Moulton Howe. He also started and funded the first year of Art Bell's *Dreamland* radio show. Bigelow is the founder of a sort of paranormal research foundation—the National Institute for Discovery Sciences. About three years ago, Bigelow purchased interview notes, transcripts, and tape recordings of abductees made by a long-time researcher, John Carpenter. Carpenter is a licensed social worker in the State of Missouri and has conducted seminars throughout the nation, aimed at providing therapy for abductees. The files sold by Carpenter to Bigelow involves about 140 families.

The first news of this sale hit the Internet at the time of the national convention of MUFON (Mutual UFO Network) this summer. John Velez, a webmaster—until earlier this year he was the webmaster for UFO researcher Budd Hopkins and his 'Intruders' website— interviewed Walt Andrus, the outgoing head of MUFON about Carpenter's sale of abductee files. Velez posted this interview on the UFO Updates message board. Carpenter responded to the message by pointing out that these were largely personal interview notes and transcripts with only the initials of the interviewees used. He underscored the fact that no video tapes were involved, although some audio tapes were (largely unintelligible, he adds). Carpenter also pointed out that his sale of the files was similar to a MUFON project (also funded by Bigelow) called the Abduction Transcription Project which involved "900 hypnosis transcripts that were collected from twenty researchers for analysis by MUFON's new computer" (Carpenter response to Velez on UFO Updates website, July 26, 2000). Andrus assured Velez that no MUFON files were involved, only Carpenter's personal files.

Within days, it was the subject of intense posting on one side or another. Some asserted that Carpenter had violated an ethical obligation to honor the privacy of abductees. Others contended that Carpenter was furthering the cause of science by selling this information to an organization with the resources to study it properly. Still, others asserted that since there is no strict field of study called UFOlogy, the whole thing comes down to entertainment and is thereby exempt from ethical considerations. Abductees interviewed by researchers began to question the ethics of the researchers who had interviewed them, and in time question the ethics of the entire field. This has been a year far different from the fun anniversary of 1997—50 years after Roswell. This has been a year when many friendships in the UFO field were broken. Some people have questioned assumptions they have had for years. Some have doubted their own memories or even sanity in their disillusionment.

Lawrence Valley Spook Lights

A few months ago, Bernice Schroder of Viroqua, formerly of La Farge, sent me a letter telling me about the famous Lawrence Valley Spook Lights, outside of LaFarge. I will quote liberally from her letter in this article about the lights:

"The 'rock' is located on property I now own and last Fall I climbed up and took pictures. (At 79, it will likely be my last trip up there)."

She encounters an old friend, Lavern Lawrence, and asks him about the mystery:

"He is the youngest son of Ezra Lawrence who lived in the log cabin in the valley…Lavern recalls a date of October 13, when the light usually appeared. He described it as that of a moon. It moved up and along the top of the 'hill'... It would reappear and follow the same path over and over as he described it. The 'hill' was now covered with trees but the light never went behind a tree. He found this significant. He remembers people coming to the valley to watch for its appearance several nights in the Fall. They were not successful but he recalls after they left it appeared. Accompanying the appearance was a strange feeling which he described as 'the hair standing up on the back of his neck'".

She recalled a description of the light seen by Don Potter:

"The story contrasts somewhat with the story Don Potter tells. He, his son Larry, and a friend were riding their mules in the valley in the fall of the year coon hunting. He describes seeing two lights resembling yard lights. They didn't seem to move. Their location seemed in the direction of 'Spook Rock' rather than 'the hill' as Lavern tells it. Don tells also of the strange, spooky, and strong urge to get out of there..."

She reflects on the cause of the lights:

"And what is my take on these apparent unusual and abnormal occurrences? I don't know! I doubt that these events would evoke scientific interest to search for an explanation. But one never knows. Could these exceptional sensory experiences affect one and not another? Is it a phenomenon related to the hill country and why limited to this one valley and one specific time of the year? I would suspect this will take its place along with UFO sightings and haunted houses. The continued experiences as in recent times with the Potters will keep the myth alive. And while one may find it fascinating, it will likely remain one of those mysteries that are unexplained and unsolved."

Local Sightings

Man from La Crosse
(taken from National UFO Reporting Center website: http://nuforc.ufoarchive.com)
Posted : 7/29/2000
Location : La Crosse, WI
Shape : Light Object appeared in telescope field of view, and executed 90 degree turn before moving out of field of view.

Object observed through telescope. Object estimated to be mag. 8.0 to 8.5, blue-white in appearance, observed for 6-8 seconds. Object observed to execute 90 degree turn in field of view of telescope, then exit field of view. Although object appeared to be similar to what a satellite looks like when it shoots across my field of view, satellites do not execute turns. Object did not slow down while turning. Entire turn took 2-3 seconds, and object observed to fly in straight lines 1-2 seconds before and after executing turn. No "running lights" observed. Thus, plus speed of turn and turn radius rule out aircraft of known kind. Turn appeared smooth. Object observed while looking for Comet Linear, approximately 8 degrees from lower "pointer" star in "big dipper" region.

Man from Viola

This was in 1969 in the Waukesha, Wis. area. It was a summer night, dark, but not late—probably at the end of August. I was looking for satellites and things. This small light about the size of a satellite came over, going about four times faster than the satellites. It went from the horizon to overhead in 15 seconds, and then shot back then shot upwards and vanished. The whole thing lasted about thirty seconds.

A Man from Tomah
from NUFORC website:
Posted : 12/16/1999
Location : Tomah, WI
Shape : Chevron/Saw a Chevron type of object with green and white lights on it. It flew very slowly across the interstate by Tomah. Witnessed by 5 other people parked along the interstate watching object.

Other witnesses were strangers parked along the interstate. Object was about 200 feet across. Moved very slowly without sound. Moved to the south east direction. Lights did not blink and were on all the time. I have driven this route on the interstate to work for 23 years and never have seen anything remotely resembling a UFO until 12-7-99. Very strange sight and traffic was heavy that night.

from NUFORC website:
Posted : 4/1/2000
Location : Madison, WI
Shape : Formation We saw 3 lights, as bright as stars in the city, move due south. They seemed to be 1000's of feet above us and moving quite fast. The very weird thing was that they oscillated rapidly in a lateral direction while moving.

My girlfriend and I stepped off of our front porch in downtown Madison, circa December 1999.

Looking straight up to see the stars, as I am wont to do, I noticed three lights in a triangular formation moving very rapidly to the South. The lights were about as bright as stars and seemed to be very high in the sky. From the time I noticed them until the time they left the horizon it was, at most, 10 seconds.

The thing that was very bizarre was that all three of the lights oscillated or "jiggled" very rapidly in a lateral direction as they flew.

A Woman from Viroqua

At Sidie Hollow Park, I walk my dog in the evenings. About three years ago, I noticed for the first time a big blue/white light that is circular in shape. This is bigger than a star but was nowhere as big as the Moon. It is not a satellite because it wobbles or dances when it moves. I don't see it every night, but at least two or three times a month.

When I see it, I think it senses that I see it, because it will come and go numerous times for a half-hour or more.

Yes, I have seen more than one at the same time. That is another part of the story.

One evening in June of this year (2000), I just had a feeling to go out there. I walked with my dog out into the center of a cornfield. This was early summer, so the corn was not knee high. I looked up and I saw three lights moving across the sky in the shape of a triangle. Then I realized that there was an enormous craft between the lights. It was like the dark sky was moving overhead. It was a beautiful night, very clear.

Then, right out of the center of the triangle came a light like the ones on the points and the ones I had seen night after night. It went out and to the left and down, and then it flew in sync with the triangle. This triangle was as big as two barns, flattened out. It was maybe a couple of hundred feet in the air. It moved very slowly. I was running in the field—why I don't know—and the triangle was barely ahead of me. I stopped running when I got to the woods. The triangle kept going southeast (towards Readstown). I saw this thing just once. But I have seen the smaller lights since then.

Man from La Crosse
from NUFORC website:
Posted: 2/16/2000
Location: La Crosse, 3 -3.5 miles south of Goose Island Park, WI
Shape: Unknown

Driving south on Hwy35, I saw what appeared to be an aircraft crossing the Mississippi River with two white lights which did not strobe. Mississippi River mile marker 691. It crossed the main channel and dropped in altitude slowed below the stall speed of an airplane, as it moved east towards Hwy 35. It stopped over Goose Island park, the southern end. I pulled over at this park entrance which I believe closes at 10:00 pm Then the two white lights went out for about 15 seconds, then moved on slowly stopped lights out, and after the third time stopped and started to descend below the tree line, and its lights went out. I drove south.

The two white lights kept at an equal distance even when turned on again, I opened my window and could hear no helicopter sound, and the lights were spaced too far apart for any helicopter fuselage. There were four cars ahead of me going south they all slowed down but no one pulled over. I wish I would have driven down to the southern end of the park where there is a boat landing. It would have been worth the fine! I believe it did land.

A Man from Readstown

In the first week of January, this year (2000), I noticed a reddish light just over the ridge southeast of Readstown. It gradually rose straight in the air and changed into a white light. Next, it began to move north away from the ridge—but very slowly. Slowly, it moved north and west, crossing the valley of Highway 14. It continued over Readstown and I lost sight of it to the west. The next day, I spoke with a woman who saw the same light, but she was farther north and could see it over Nelson's Hill (to the west of Readstown). She said that it came from the southeast and then hovered back and forth for some time over Nelson's Hill. It finally disappeared behind the hill.

Chinese UFOs and Space Projects

A wave of UFO sightings in China has attracted attention to the growing Chinese UFOlogy movement. In fact, the first UFO sighting of the Millennium was reported in China and even recorded by TV cameras:

"At about 6:30 am, Beijing time on Saturday, January 1, 2000, a silver-gray UFO appeared over the Great Wall of China. As it hovered, it was captured by Cable News network (CNN) TV cameras and broadcast live in the USA. Eyewitness M. Lamb was watching the CNN coverage "when CNN showed a shot of the Great Wall of China at sunrise...When they cut to the shot, there was a gray orb floating over the wall. Then it floated to the right, then up. Then they (CNN) cut away from the shot without any explanation of the floating object. It was silver and appeared to float or glide without any means of propulsion." (UFO Roundup/ Joseph Trainor, editor, Vol. 5, No. 1)

A former translator for Chairman Mao, Sun Shili, has founded the Chinese UFO Research Organization, which now has a membership of 40,000 including professors, students, engineers, and even Communist party members. Sun reports there are over 3,000 UFO sightings in China each year.

China has also announced the formation of a program somewhat like S.E..T.I. (Search for Extraterrestrial Intelligence) organization, which will scan the skies for radio signals from outer space. It has also been reported that within two decades China wants to build a reusable launcher like the Space Shuttle and begin to colonize the Moon. Japan has also launched a probe to Mars called Nozumi ("Hope"), which is expected to reach the Red Planet in January 2004.

2001 UFO EVENTS

The aftermath of the September 11, 2001 terrorist attacks in New York City and Washington, D.C., resulted in most aircraft being grounded for days throughout the United States. It was pointed out at the time, that if there ever were a time when the existence of UFOs as truly extraterrestrial craft could be verified then this was indeed it. And there were numerous sightings of various kinds of craft throughout the USA on September 11 and on the days afterward:

The following report came from a person in Griffin, Georgia:

"I AM VERY SERIOUS ABOUT THIS REPORT. I do not know what this means but I was getting home from band practice tonight, the night that all the crashes happened. I was looking around the sky for the light of planes because I knew they were supposed to be grounded. I looked to the north and saw two disks with lights on the edge through some clouds. They had lights on them that changed in sync from blue to green. They darted around each other for about 10-15 seconds before I lost track of them. I was really freaked out and I felt like this needed to be shared." from the National UFO Reporting Center website: http://www.nwlink.com/~ufocntr/ .

The following report, dated Sept. 11, came from someone in Massachusetts:

(Who observed extremely bizarre air activities near Boston's Logan Airport—one of the departure points of the terrorist attackers—)

"Logan had been shut due to trade center attack. We had witnessed fighter jets all day. I live in a small neighborhood just outside Logan. Noticed a star-like object in the eastern sky. Ran home to get a video camera and Father. Upon return we were greeted by 4 others who were also observing the sky over short beach, upon zooming in with my Sony Digital 8 handcam, I noticed an object that appeared to be still in the sky, but by binocular it seemed to dance all around There were blue and red lights that were moving all around the craft. We then witnessed what appeared to be something that looked like Mitosis, the splitting of a vessel into two parts. One object's lights began to move rapidly in a different pattern as if to be communicating with the other ship. One looked as if it was a firework, and then quickly disappeared, and reappeared to the left at a 45 degree angle. We then witnessed a triangle-type formation with yet another craft. I have all sorts of footage, although craft appeared to disappear and reappear frequently. Craft were also rapidly moving west to east. Very intense. Then we also witnessed 3 fighter jets flying to and above these objects. Video footage played in slow motion shows the intricate light pattern on one ship, also looks to have very bright lights in the center and almost force field-like arcs moving from the center to the outer edges of the object. Many people stopped vehicles to get out and see it. Not many clouds in the sky. What are these ships, has anyone else seen them?"

September 11 UFO Sightings

On September 11 alone, about 20 UFO sightings were reported throughout the USA, many of which were extremely similar and detailed, and two of which report military or aircraft flying nearby. An interesting sighting is reported from Wisconsin a few days later, on September 15:

"For some reason, I woke up around 4 am and couldn't sleep. So, still laying down in the bed I was staring through the window at the stars. Several minutes later suddenly I saw a strange object passing the skies from north to south. It looked like two yellowish spheres which were interconnected by invisible bonds. I immediately woke up my wife screaming 'Look UFO!' And she saw this thing also. She was shocked. I jumped out of my bed and rushed for the video camera. I was concerned about the time and therefore worked quickly. It was pretty cold outside and the grass was very wet, in spite I was barefooted and shaking I was able to locate the object and pointed the camera at it. Unfortunately, the camcorder screen blinked once and that showed low battery indicator. I was so upset. Soon object vanished soundlessly and I returned back home. Couple days before I was recording my kids on camera and completely forgot to charge the battery. Rest of the night we couldn't sleep discussing this event." This came from Portage, Wisconsin.

From Soldiers Grove
(this report was posted on the National UFO Reporting Center website)

"It started off with a huge flash we now know was an Iridium flash (east of our place). Then my friend saw a beam of light in the sky (which I didn't see). The first "craft" appeared right where the iridium flash disappeared. It looked like a disc with flashing lights of blue, violet, red, green white. All of these light colors were on each of these ships. There looked like one light of each color on each of these, but they mostly flashed two at a time. This craft was "hovering" there, sitting in one spot but sort of moving back and forth just a bit. Then it shot off to the west very quickly. It took about two seconds to cross the sky and disappear. Then from the west (not from one particular spot) more came, 1 or 2 at a time. They looked just like the first one, 20-30 total (I wasn't counting so I am unsure of this). They traveled at the same speed to the east to the spot where the iridium flash had been. They each started to slow down right before they got to this spot, almost to a stop. It slowly went behind the tree (I could see it through the leaves) and right when it came out from behind the tree they disappeared. Two airplanes did fly over right after it ended, and they weren't anything like the craft. I'm not sure if they were chasing them or not."

A Readstown couple report at about the same time (reported to me)

"I was a passenger in a car with my husband returning from La Crosse one evening this summer between nine and ten o'clock. We were on Highway 14 at the top of the hill before Coon Valley. We saw an intense white light to the southwest. It reminded my husband of the glow of a welding torch. It never turned any colors. it wasn't like lightning. It was flashing up from the ground. They would be in one spot for a time, then somewhere else for a moment later, then somewhere else again. We never saw any kind of object. Just these lights. We don't think it was fireworks. Later on, we saw it when we climbed the next hill between Coon Valley and Westby, later between Westby and Viroqua—always to the southwest. Finally, we saw it one last time as we left Viroqua, straight ahead, like it was over Readstown."

Other Local Sightings

Reports continue—this one originating in Florence County in Northern Wisconsin just a couple of weeks ago on Oct. 20, 2001:

"I was outdoors looking east towards Gemini. I noticed a small "star" rising over the trees across the lake. It kept rising and falling below the tree line. It rose further and moved left to right. After a while, it was joined by another object. These both moved closer to my location. They were both moving left to right and would sometimes disappear. They kept getting closer, and higher in the sky, perhaps 20 degrees. After about 20 minutes, they were quite close to my location and a third "star-like" object appeared probably about 1000 ft in front of me. at about 40 degrees. This last object was pulsating like someone using a "dimmer" switch. It also grew larger and smaller. The three objects hovered in a triangle formation. I left the scene as I was a little "spooked" by all this. I didn't sleep well and have had some very "funny" dreams."

This was posted on the new Wisconsin UFO website— UFO Wisconsin: http://ufowisconsin.com/

This site alleges that Wisconsin has the second-highest number of UFO sightings of any state in the union—they say that only New Mexico has more. This site also provides a link to the new American Science Fiction and UFO Museum which has recently opened in Wisconsin Dells: http://www.ufomuseum.com/

The site also provides a link to Belleville, Wisconsin, which bills itself as the UFO Capital of the World: http://www.angelfire.com/wi/grogan/belleville.html

2002 UFO EVENTS

The UFO cause was given a recent boost when President Clinton's former Chief of Staff joined with the Sci-Fi channel in an effort to release government UFO files.

(from *Filers Files* website)

Date: Wed, 23 Oct 2002 12:50:41 -0400

"UFO DISCLOSURE CLINTON'S CHIEF OF STAFF JOHN PODESTA WASHINGTON—SCI FI Channel is supporting a new effort to gain the release of secret government records on unidentified aerial phenomena. John Podesta, former Clinton White House Chief of Staff, spoke in an attempt to gain the release of secret government UFO records. He cited the importance to the public of declassifying government UFO records. Clinton's Science Advisor Dr. John Gibbons initiated an investigation by the USAF into the crash of an unknown object at Roswell, New Mexico. Clinton's first CIA Director James Woolsey in 1993 also green-lighted a new CIA investigation into UFOs. Clinton himself asked his good friend Webster Hubbell to find out the truth about UFOs. Hillary

Clinton, also very interested in the UFO phenomena, helped Laurance Rockefeller edit a letter to President Clinton on UFOs, and was briefed on the UFO subject by Rockefeller at the Rockefeller ranch during the President's 1995 vacation there. The Coalition for Freedom of Information (C! FI) is requesting documents involving Project Moon Dust and Operation Blue Fly, clandestine operations reported to have existed decades ago to investigate UFOs and retrieve objects of unknown origins. The Podesta statement is part of an announcement by the SCI FI Channel in support of a new effort to gain the release of secret government records. The big announcement was made at the National Press Club in Washington on October 22, 2002."

Local Sightings

A Woman from Vernon County

This spring, I was driving at night on Highway 27 north of Westby. I had been heading south. Suddenly to my left (to the east) I saw some lights. It kind of had a pyramid or triangular shape. It had multiple, colored lights. It was moving north and continued so until I lost sight of it. I saw it for more than a couple of minutes.

UFOWisconsin Report

A Readstown Person
Date: October 13, 2002 2:03AM
Location: Potosi
County: Grant
Source: UFOWisconsin Report Form Submission - Witness

requested to remain anonymous

"I was driving north on Hwy 61 between Dickeyville and Potosi/Tennyson. About one mile outside of Tennyson, I observed a flashing toward the Mississippi. It was not the usual barge lights. I thought to myself that a new cellular tower must be up down there as I could only see the sky flashing and not the source. A little further down the road, I looked over Hog Hollow toward the river and saw five red lights shaped like an inverted V. After about three seconds they were gone. This was above the hollow. There are no roads, not even field roads to access the hollow. The river is not visible from this location so it could not have been anything on it. I grew up there and I have never observed anything like this before."

From NUFORC website:
Occured : 8/2/2002 23:30 (Entered as : 8-02 23:30)
Reported : 9/10/2002 8:00:59 pm 20:00
Posted : 9/13/2002
Location : Osseo, WI
Shape : Disk spinning craft with green aura circling above.

My son who is 10 claims to have seen a saucer-shaped object circling above. He said it had a green aura and the craft spun inside this aura. He said the green light would get real bright then be gone and start all over again. Also, the craft had bright white lights around its perimeter. I'm not sure what to think, most would say active imagination, but he is pretty freaked out about it. He has a classmate that described the same thing to him, so I don't know what to think. Just wondering if anyone else has seen something like this, or if I should just sum it up to imagination.

((NUFORC Note: Date in August is approximate. PD))

Occurred: 7/21/2002 09:04 (Entered as : 07/21/2002 9:04 p.m)
Reported: 7/21/2002 3:21:27 pm 15:21
Posted: 7/26/2002
Location: Dundee, WI
Shape: Light Numerous lights maneuvering and making formation

We were gathered at Benson's Hideaway in Dundee, Wisconsin on Saturday night July 21, 2002.

There were a number of people outside enjoying the beautiful summer evening. The sky was overcast and there were a few lightning strikes to the west, but there were clearer skies to the north and east. As I began to take a bite into a sandwich, a bright orange/white light rose up over the northern horizon. The lights were about half the size of my thumb at arm's length.

A total of five lights appeared and maneuvered into a formation. They all began directly north of us and floated (without any sound) into a formation northeast of us out over Long Lake. Two or three times, one light made numerous flashes. After a few minutes, one by one, the lights blinked out.

About fifteen minutes later, 3 smaller lights silently floated over our heads from south to north in a span of about 1-3 minutes.

There were 2 green lights with a red light in the middle. As the lights passed overhead, they also made no sound and were moving back and forth in relation to one another. I have a video of the first formation of lights.

A Giant Egg in Wisconsin Dells
(witnessed by many)

Occurred : 6/28/2002 21:00 (Entered as : 06/28/02 21:00)
Reported : 9/11/2002 6:40:57 am 06:40
Posted : 9/13/2002
Location : Wisconsin Dells, WI
Shape : Egg/ A giant egg shape, trails moving slowly side to side and left after a couple minutes

"I was in Wisconsin Dells, WI, on 06/28/02 at 9:00 pm, I looked at the sky, and this giant circle "egg shape" was rotating real fast and was moving side to side for about two minutes, and just after that this UFO disappeared in front of everyone's eyes, many witnesses were watching this event."

Madison Tube
Occurred: 6/1/2002 14:00 (Entered as: 06/01/02 14:00)
Reported: 6/4/2002 11:25:25 am 11:25
Posted: 6/12/2002
Location: Madison, WI
Shape: Cylinder Tubular Shape and Glinting Object

"Tubular shape coming from the north and going to the south. I saw it for a moment as I was distracted by another object "glinting" traveling from the south to the north. "Glinting" object seemed to travel to the north changing direction unlike a plane or a helicopter. "Glinting" object entered a cloud and continued to "glint" when I noticed the tubular shape coming from the north. I originally thought it was a plane as there is an airport north of town. When I looked back a couple of seconds later...it had disappeared as had the "glinting" object."

Circles Rendezvous
Occurred: 4/13/2002 12:20 (Entered as 04/13/02 1220)
Reported: 4/15/2002 8:18:18 am 08:18
Posted: 4/25/2002
Location: Muskego, WI
Shape: Circle UFO's rendezvous over SE Wisconsin Sat April 13th, 2002. 1220 pm

"Sat., April 13th, 2002 at approximately 1220 CST, my wife returned from the grocery store. I went outside to sneak up on her. As I was approaching her, I looked up to the North and saw two airplanes, one flying South and banking East to make an approach to Mitchell airfield. The other was much higher and heading North West leaving behind it a vapor trail. Immediately upon fixing my eyes on those airplanes I saw a small circle-shaped grayish colored object streak across the sky in a Westerly direction. I tried to get my wife to see it but she looked toward the direction of the airplanes and discounted what I had to say. With my eyes fixed on this new object, I walked around the back of the cars to get a better look. This object was flying in a straight line, and the only noise I heard was from the first airplane which was on approach. The UFO was smaller than either airplane and was traveling quite fast. Also, it was not leaving a vapor trail. As this object was flying away to a point West of my location it suddenly started to turn, but I didn't notice a banking movement as with the airplane. It started making complete counter-clockwise circles along the same altitude it was flying, and I made a mental note of how small the flight radius was for such a fast speed. Well, within a few seconds there appeared a second object, and then a third and a fourth. They were all flying in counter-clockwise circles stacked over the same airspace separated by altitude. The objects were going in and out of view as if they were reflecting off of the sun and then not and then reflecting again. I estimate watching this for about five minutes when my eyes became strained from the sunlight and I desperately wanted to go get the video camera. So I went inside and got the camera but when I went back outside I could not find the objects anymore. There were no news reports of any unusual flying objects. The weather was sunny, unlimited visibility, 59 degrees F, dew point was 43 degrees F, with a few upper-level clouds in the distance."

Circle object with very bright lights.
Occurred: 2/2/2002 06:05 (Entered as 2/2/02 6:05 am)
Reported : 2/2/2002 5:37:15 am 05:37
Posted: 2/22/2002
Location: Eau Claire, WI
Shape: Circle object with very bright lights.

"I was driving home this morning, and I noticed some lights ahead I slowed down and the image appeared circular and metallic. there were lights that seemed to rotate and the craft had a kind of mirror effect to it. I was about 50 feet away from it.it shot straight up very fast and then was gone. there seemed to be a kind of electric charge in the air. I am not sure what it was but it was nothing I have never seen before. I am a 31-year-old female and I have little to no information on UFOs so I could be wrong with what I thought it was."

Triangle Low Flying
Occurred: 5/13/2002 21:15 (Entered as 5/13/02 21:15)
Reported : 5/13/2002 8:24:36 pm 20:24
Posted: 5/14/2002
Location: Mosinee, WI
Shape: triangular craft seen near airport.

"Me and my friend were driving down the road and we looked up and saw two bright white lights above a field. We wondered if it was just a pole or something else. As we got closer, we saw there was a red flickering light in the middle. We pulled over and watched whatever it was and it looked like it hovered. It all of the sudden took off back toward town. I rolled down the window and listened to it. It sounded somewhat like a lawnmower. We turned around and followed it. We were going about 55 or 60 mph and it was speeding way ahead of us. We thought it might be a plane because there was an airport (Central Wisconsin Airport) that way but couldn't figure out why it was so low and why it was going so fast. As we kept going, we saw it hovering over a field again. We saw that it looked triangular and somewhat flat. We pulled over and watched it again. It took off once again and we saw yellow lights now. As we followed it back the other way, it looked like it dipped and crossed the road and hovered about 50 or 70 ft above a house. We reached up with it again, pulled over, and watched it again. This time, it took off very fast and looked like it landed in a field somewhere or something up ahead but it was too fast to see where it went or landed."
((NUFORC Note: We will request a written report from the other student-witness. Please see other report from Holland, MI, for this date and approximate time. PD))

Triangle Transparent
Occurred: 10/22/2001 00:35 (Entered as 10/22/01 24:35)
Reported: 10/26/2001 1:06:09 pm 13:06
Posted: 11/20/2001
Location: Verona, WI
Shape: Triangle Transparent object of unknown origin, exhibiting previously unknown capabilities, appears overhead.

"October 22, 2001, 12:35 am I was looking straight up in the sky when I noticed that the sky appeared to be moving. I looked closer, and noticed a triangular object that appeared to be transparent, and outlined in lights. The lights were 1/2-1/4 the light of the nearest stars. The body of the craft moved from the 90-degree angle that it first appeared to me, to approx. 45 degrees on the Southern horizon before disappearing (it became too hard to see—it did not speed off). The body of the craft fluctuated, acting as if it were floating atop the waves in the ocean. The lights all appeared to be fixed to the craft and moved in unison with the body. The craft appeared to be bigger than a full moon in size. The craft appeared to be moving steadily, and my view of it lasted approximately 7 seconds. What was interesting, is that it seemed like you could look through the body of the craft, and see the sky behind it."

1900 Object
"Around three o'clock one morning in the summer of 1900, as he was returning from a dance in a rural area near Reedsburg, Wisconsin, 14-year-old P.A. McGilvra stopped his horse atop a small hill. The animal seemed to be disturbed by something in the densely wooded area,

and as McGilvra searched for the cause, he happened to look up into a cloudless sky brilliant with stars. There he saw the outline of an enormous dark, dirigible-shaped vehicle.

The object passed at a low altitude over some nearby poplar trees, and as it did so, the trunks of the trees bent dramatically as if in reaction to a strong wind, but no wind was blowing. When the object flew over the witness' head, he heard a loud swishing sound. Soon the UFO was out of sight, but the horse remained frightened for some time. When interviewed many years later, McGilvra said that the other local people had had similar experiences around the same time."

Jerome Clark. *The UFO Book: Encyclopedia of the Extra-terrestrial*, Detroit, MI: Visible Ink Press, 1997.

Elroy Woman Held Hostage: Has Important Message for President Clinton (1995)

In early June, 1995, an Elroy police officer and Juneau County sheriff's deputy responded to a report of a woman being held hostage in her home.

Hostage situations are always tense, dangerous.

Fortunately for the two officers involved, there were no negotiations, no shots fired, and no one injured. The woman's captors weren't your typical hostage-takers. No foreign nationals, no jail-breaking cons seeking a place to hole up for a while, and no crazed ex-husband or enraged child returned, bent on revenge.

None of that 10 o'clock news drama stuff.

The woman's captors were aliens from the planet Uranus.

When the officers entered the woman's apartment,

they found her perched on the kitchen table. She expressed alarm at the prospect of descending from her place of safety. Better on the table than on the floor.

In a quick search of the apartment, the officers were unable to find any aliens, either hiding or in plain view. They did find the woman's 9-year-old daughter.

Nothing here. It was safe to come down, they told her.

Coaxed down from her perch, the woman told the officers that she was doing research on black magic and on the existence of life on other planets. She was also psychic, she said and conceded that she may not have been held physically captive, but only receiving a vision. The aliens hadn't yet landed nor taken her captive; instead, she was experiencing a vision of things to come.

She then rushed to the phone. "Excuse me, I've got to call someone quick," she told the officers. She dialed a long-distance number.

When the call was answered on the other end, she asked to speak to President Clinton.

The notebook in front of her included phone numbers for the U.S. State Department, the White House, and for the National Emergency Concerning Oceans and Nuclear Warfare.

Finishing her call, the woman relayed to the officers that she does not give psychic readings for the benefit of others. She said she devoted all of her psychic talents for the sole purpose of conducting research for the exclusive use of President Bill Clinton.

The Elroy police officer called the Department of Human Services to alert them to the woman's condition. At the woman's request, she asked Human Services to put her and her daughter up in a local hotel.

She knew that if she remained in her home the aliens would take over her body. And they'd use her body to get into the White House.

Source: "Officers Aid Woman Who Fears Aliens," Unattributed, Juneau County Star-Times [Mauston], Thursday, June 22, 1995

Story Credit: Richard Heiden

Copyright 2001 Weird Wisconsin

From UFO Roundup, Oct. 2002

UFOs Are Active Again in Wisconsin

On Wednesday, October 9, 2002, Carmen K. reported, "My husband and I went outside around 8:30 pm. to observe some strange lights in the sky" near their home in Wisconsin Rapids, Wis. (population 18,435), a town located 75 miles (120 kilometers) west of Green Bay. "When I got outside, I saw what appeared to be a falling star and I told him that's what I thought it was. At that point, two objects became apparent and began flashing like strobe lights. At first, they were white in color when they were moving from east to west. Then they looped around and within seconds were back in the same spot I had first seen them... We called out my parents and our son, and we all observed them for around 30 more minutes. At one point, we saw as many as five of the lights, ranging in color from white to red. When they were red, the lights were steady and not flashing like the rest of them... A plane then flew overhead, and the lights seemed to follow and come up on the plane very quickly like they were observing the plane. Then they disappeared for a few minutes and reappeared in the same spot I had first seen them. There was absolutely no noise with the objects."

Later on, Sunday, October 13, 2002, at 10:35 pm, eyewitness P.G.L. was at home in West Allis, Wis. (population 61,254), a suburb of Milwaukee, when he noticed a strange light in the sky. "I stopped at our skylight just before bed and was looking at what I thought was the constellation Cassiopeia, but then, just below it, suddenly appeared four orange triangles," P.G.L. reported. (Editor's Comment: Perhaps the same four triangular UFOs seen in Northampton, UK last week!) "They appeared to be hovering approximately 1,000 feet (300 meters) up, and then moved at first slowly and then very quickly in a southeasterly direction. Since our skylight is on a slanted part of our roof, I was able to observe them for approximately 10 more seconds... The configuration was three triangles in the same of an arrowhead, with a fourth riding underneath the arrowhead." The fourth UFO "and the right tip of the arrowhead appeared to veer off slightly, still staying with the group, as they flew off at a greater rate of speed, due south until I could no longer see them." (Many thanks to John Hoppe of UFO Wisconsin for these reports.)

2003 UFO EVENTS

The UFO season in the Kickapoo Valley has been rather slow except for a number of reports of what was clearly the planet Mars earlier this year on August 27, 2003, making its closest approach to Earth in 60,000 years. Throughout the world, many early risers saw a large red shape in the southern sky for a couple of weeks. Numerous UFO websites received reports of this natural space phenomenon. The event prompted thinking about Mars as a target for space exploration and as a possible home of a lost civilization. The Space Shuttle disaster in February put the U.S. space program on hold for at least a year. The recent Chinese launching of its first "tyconaut" was a reminder that space will not belong to just the Russians and the Americans. The Chinese have speculated on a Moon landing within a decade.

UFO over Lake Superior

November 2003 will mark the 50th anniversary of a mysterious UFO event that took place which involved Wisconsin. On November 23, 1953, an F-89c airplane based in Madison took off from Sault St. Marie, Michigan to pursue a UFO over Lake Superior. The radar screen showed the plane approach a radar blip which had suddenly appeared over the Soo Locks.

"Our jet zeroed in on this object at 500 miles per hour. We watched the blips on the scope. The two blips merged. Then there was nothing. We've been unable to establish radio contact with the plane and presume it's lost." Said an officer of Kinross Air Base. The UFO continued on its: "the radar return from the other aircraft (the UFO) indicated it was continuing on its original flight path, while the return from the F-89 disappeared."

These quotes come from the *W-Files* by Jay Rath (who has Kickapoo Valley connections). The reaction of the military to the incident was almost as mysterious as the incident itself. Rath says the U.S. military initially tried to blame the incident on a mid-air collision with a Canadian plane known to have been flying in the area. However, the Canadians firmly denied this.

No trace was ever found of the plane or its two occupants. Charges of a cover-up were raised in 1957 by UFO investigator Major Donald E. Keyhoe, a retired Marine officer: "The Air Force should tell us the results of their investigation... What was the unknown? I say the evidence points to a midair collision between the F-89 and something else. What was that object? Where did it come from?" (from *W-Files*, page 100). Madison's *Capital Times* attempted to investigate the matter in 1957, and were met with this response:

"Don't get your readers all steamed up about these things. It will only mean that we'll start getting a flood of sightings from Wisconsin that will cost the Air Force a lot of taxpayer's money to investigate... Lots of atmospheric conditions cause blips on radar... And lots of planes go down."

By coincidence, Oct. 2003 marked the 25th anniversary of a similar incident in Australia. On Oct 21, 1978, a man named Fredrick Valentich radioed in a report about a strange craft hovering over his Cessna: "...and the thing is just orbiting on top of me. Also, it's got a green light and sort of metallic. It's shiny (on) the outside."

The object suddenly disappeared from sight and then came back into his view: "...that strange aircraft is hovering on top of me again... It is hovering and it is not an aircraft."

Then there were 17 seconds of open mike followed by a loud scraping sound. Then silence. No trace of Valentich or his plane was ever found.

Wisconsin Crop Circle

A crop circle, which was talked about and studied worldwide, appeared on July 4, 2003, near Mayville, Wisconsin. A group of investigators were sent to the crop circle by MUFON (Mutual UFO Network) who studied the formation thoroughly. They recorded an eyewitness account:

"Art Rantala, a retired truck driver, on July 4, 2003, at approximately 7:30 am. Central Daylight Time (CDT) was up early making coffee in his workshop and watching a weather front that was moving across the Dodge County, Wisconsin area. His workshop is located a few miles from the town of Mayville and the village of Kekoskee, and situated on top of a hill overlooking a wheat field owned by a Mrs. Schaufnagel and farmed by a third party...

"Art poured his first cup of coffee at 7:35 am. CDT noticing the time on his coffee maker.

"A few minutes later (approx. 7:40 am. CDT) as the rain was falling, the wind picked up and Rantala noticed that the bark began flying off a hickory nut tree that was about 10 feet outside his open, east-facing workshop window.

"He leaned out the window to take a closer look. Rantala then noticed that directly across the street a group of trees "started swinging every which way." He said that as he followed the trees blowing around, his gaze naturally followed down to the wheat field where the circles appeared one by one in front of him.

"The northernmost circle farthest from the road (what we have named Circle #1 in order of appearance), formed first, appearing as a 'black hole' in the standing wheat that was created when the circle of wheat was flattened down. Next, the southern-most circle closest to the road formed (Circle #2), followed by the one in the center (Circle #3). Rantala said all the circles were flattened in roughly 12 seconds, but no more than 15 seconds. Rantala's important eyewitness observation to the crop circles forming may be the first ever recorded in the USA, and is certainly one of the only a couple of dozen reported worldwide in the last 50 years. Rantala reported that there were no apparent means for the wheat to have been swirled and flattened—nothing unusual in the sky, no lights, no unusual sounds, and no unusual odors. Whatever the energetic force was that caused the circles to form it was beyond the range of visible sight."

Local Sightings

From National UFO Reporting Center:
Occurred: 2/8/2002 05:30 (Entered as 02/08/2002 5:30)
Reported: 1/6/2007 12:02:47 pm 12:02
Posted: 2/1/2007
Location: Beloit/Milwaukee (between), WI
Shape: Changing
Duration: approximately 1 hour the object appeared cigar-shaped and emitted strobe light patterns of various colors.

I reported this incident back in 2002, at which time it was posted on your website and also on the Wisconsin website (taken from yours). It remained there for some time. When I had not checked on it for a couple of years, I found that it had been erased. I'm not sure why it was erased unless it was deemed incredible. However, the recent sighting at O'Hare reinforces the accuracy of my family's UFO sighting that took place in February 2002.

I am a former teacher and substitute teacher, and my husband is an Air Force veteran and a retired IRS Special Agent, who is currently employed as an inspector for the Illinois State Police.

As to the incident, my husband, along with our 13-year-old daughter, and myself, witnessed a UFO for approximately one hour while driving east on Highway 43 between Beloit, WI. and Milwaukee, WI. at approximately 5:30 am. in February 2002. The object first came into view as an unusual very bright light in the clear sky south of our position. At this time in the morning, the sky was completely dark and we continually observed this object as it appeared to move closer to our position.

As we traveled eastbound on Highway 43, the object

began to take shape. We had no idea how far away the UFO was, but it eventually began traveling in parallel to our vehicle. When it first became identifiable, it appeared to be cigar-shaped, with a lighted opaque dome.

From time to time, the object emitted various light patterns consisting of various colored lights in a strobe-light format. As the object came closer to us, it seemed very large. The object would occasionally stop moving and fall behind our vehicle, then suddenly dart very far ahead. At one point, the object was directly parallel with our vehicle and began to turn about its axis.

The object's appearance resembled the classic description of a "Flying Saucer". Across the middle of the object were strobe lights running in a pattern of red, green, and blue lights. At various times, white, red, green, blue, and lavender-colored lights were emitted, in strobe form, from various positions on the craft.

As we came into downtown Milwaukee, the object appeared to be over the southern part of the city near the Milwaukee airport. Daybreak was taking place and the object was quite clear.

At that point, as an aircraft took off from the airport in a southwestern direction, the object rapidly climbed at a steep angle (approximately 70 degrees) in the clear sky and disappeared into a high cloud bank. This occurred at a speed far in excess of any known aircraft and similar to the O'Hare sighting.

((NUFORC Note: Date of sighting may be approximate, although the witness does not indicate that fact. PD))

2004 UFO EVENTS

Two UFO figures die in 2004

John Mack (October 4, 1929–September 27, 2004)

John Mack was a psychiatrist at the Harvard Medical School who made a study of alien abductions using hypnosis. In 1994, he published *Abduction*, a book that attracted much support and criticism. While he was initially skeptical about the phenomenon, he soon came to regard the information obtained from the hypnosis to be important:

"In a 1994 interview, Jeffrey Mishlove stated that Mack seemed 'inclined to take these [abduction] reports at face value'. Mack replied by saying, 'Face value I wouldn't say. I take them seriously. I don't have a way to account for them.'"

Mack studied hypnosis sessions with more than 200 people. He came to believe that the abduction experiences were as much spiritual as physical, therefore he came to be criticized by people such as Budd Hopkins who took a much more nuts and bolts view of the UFO phenomenon.

In 1999, he published *Passport to the Cosmos: Human Transformation and Alien Encounters*, which studied the philosophical, spiritual, and world view nature of UFOs and abduction.

In 1994, Harvard launched an investigation into Mack's use of hypnosis, questioning whether it was proper scientific method. After months of hearings and study, the university backed down from disciplining Mack, a tenured professor, and asserted that he had the academic right to study what he wanted. Legal experts such as Alan Dershowitz, Roderick Macleish, and Daniel Sheehan assisted him. Laurence Rockefeller, a longtime UFO advocate provided financial help. Numerous academics regarded the investigation as an assault on academic freedom.

In 1977, Mack had won the Pulitzer Prize in biography, for his life of T.E. Lawrence (Lawrence of Arabia). In September 2004, Mack was in London to speak to the T.E. Lawrence Society. While walking home from dinner one evening, he was struck and killed by a drunken driver.

Betty Hill (June 28, 1919–October 23, 2004)

Betty and Barney Hill are sometimes called the first UFO abductees. However, that is not quite true. Published accounts of people being abducted by the occupants of UFOs go back to the 19th century. Prior to that, there is the literature of people being taken away by fairies and other dwellers of the folklore world. Nevertheless, the September 19, 1961 encounter that the Hills had with a flying saucer and its short (4 to 5 feet), gray-skinned, human-like occupants, was the first account to achieve wide publicity in the press, motion pictures, and television.

As is the case with numerous other abductees, bad dreams and odd memories led to their seeking out the help of a hypnotist who examined both of them separately. Gradually, the story emerged of the couple being stopped on the highway, at night on the way home to Boston from a vacation in New Hampshire, by two men who took them into the woods to a waiting metallic disc. Upon entering the disc, both Hills were examined medically by the entities.

They were a mixed-race couple who was active in the civil rights movement. Barney was Black of Ethiopian descent; Betty was of English heritage. Barney worked as a postal worker and he died of a stroke in 1969 at the age of 46. Betty was a social worker and in later years she toured the country speaking at UFO conventions. She died of cancer at the age of 85.

In 1966, John Fuller wrote a book about the event called *The Interrupted Journey*. In 1995, Betty wrote a book entitled *A Common Sense Guide to UFOs*. This was their only experience with alien entities; however, Betty did see numerous UFOs in the sky in later years.

Her view of the encounter remained very upbeat and positive all her life.

"Don't be afraid," she once wrote reassuringly. "They don't hurt anybody. If they wanted to conquer us, they could."

Local Sightings

From Whence it Came

Sooo...here I sit, wondering if I'll once again miss another deadline for the annual UFOs of the Kickapoo issue. It is certainly not my intention to do so. And with that, I shall begin.

In the Fall of 1978, I began to realize the honor and privilege to serve as a caretaker for several properties in northern Richland County, Wisconsin. It was a time to be out, on and in the edge of the Ocooch Mountains observing from several places; a time, I knew, I might never have again.

Back then I preferred to work in silence, darkness, and solitude of the deep woods, away from the clutter and distractions of electrical power lines, etc.

In 1991, while residing at the garden of harmonious delights. I came to realize that it was mid-November, the time of the famous Leonid meteor showers.

It has been written that the Leonids have been known to display a shower of streaming lights, the likes of no other. It's been said that perhaps as many as 500,000 streaks of wonder occasionally adorn the darkness of the heavens at this time.

I decided to invite several of my friends and acquaintances to join me to watch for the meteors. I specifically remember inviting Liz Was, but as usual, no one came, and I was to be once again alone in my loneliness. But since I am used to this, I reveled in my chance to be by myself; to be entertained that way again.

As the darkness approached, I gathered my coat and blankets to keep me comfortable in the chill of the fall's damp air. The night was clear and perfect for viewing the cloudless sky.

I took up a position at the property's fire pit on a flat about 88 feet and valley floor. I munched on some trail mix and anxiously waited. I remember that the birds of the night were very still and quiet.

I gazed to the south toward the hillside, which was about 200 feet from me, and the top of which was over 200 feet above me. I remained silent.

Several hours passed. I saw many meteors, and then something occurred which I will never forget. Suddenly, I saw a faint, yet light green glow in the sky that covered the entire length of the hillside and showed through and slightly above the almost leafless trees. Then to my shock, awe and wonderment there appeared a sight along the base of the ridgeline.

I can only describe it this way. It was as if there were 3,000 folks in the woods with very bright flashlights pointed my way. The entire ridgeline was lit up, all 1,667 feet of it. And then in perfect unison, the lights moved slowly upward, through and then above the trees. It was like that scene from the movie *ET—the Extraterrestrial*, only much more real, vivid, and absolutely amazing.

I stood transfixed. Again, suddenly, all the lights were gone.

I immediately assumed that this had been an event of the Leonids, but then realized that meteor showers do not occur in this fashion.

Throughout all this, all my surroundings remained utterly silent. I felt calm and totally at ease, such as I often do when I am alone in the darkness and stillness of a southwestern Wisconsin night.

Several days later, a neighbor down the road stopped me and asked me what all the noise was about a few nights earlier that he had heard coming from the direction of my humble abode. I shrugged my shoulders and continued walking along, as I often do.

And with that, I shall conclude. Be patient with the farmer, for he hath many things to do. Be not frightened by the mysterious events bestowed upon us from the heavens. Interpretations are often only gestures. "Silent knowledge cannot be reasoned out. It can only be experienced."

In this planet of distress; long since incubated and sent off from who or what knows where?

Keep looking up!

Sending out A.S.O.S

Horse and Colt Visitor?

It was Saturday night, about 8:15 pm. I had just stepped outside onto the deck as my wife and I were relaxing after spending the day at the annual Horse and Colt Show on Saturday, September 25.

My wife joined me on the deck when we witnessed a white light appear out of nowhere and go zipping across the night sky. It went in a straight line from west to east.

At first, we thought it was possibly a satellite. We've watched many satellites cut across the night sky, but this light was too close for that.

We then thought it to be an airplane—but there was no noise to accompany it. My wife stepped back into the house to get the binoculars, but by the time she returned it had vanished. And I don't mean it went behind a hillside—it was too high for that and it did not go behind any clouds because there were none.

What was it—a Horse and Colt Show visitor?

Wisconsin Sightings

Occurred 12/22/2003 18:00 (entered as 12/22/2003 18:00
Reported 2/6/2004 8:59:01 am
Posted in NUFORC 2/12/2004
Location: Madison, Wis.
Shape: Other
Duration: 20 seconds shape—changing brown "tarp"

I've finally decided to send this in after hearing of two other similar UFO descriptions in the last month on Unknowncountry.com. One was about a dark-colored form changing parachute-like (not the round kind but the more oblong or oval ones) and the other a brownish jellyfish-like one that appeared to be "swimming". The one I saw, I at first thought to be an orangeish-brown tarp or plastic sheet that had been blown up into the wind and was just blowing along while slowing undulating or changing shape as though made of a very light material. And it very steadily traveled in its general direction, from north to south over the Isthmus/Willy St. area (Unfortunately, I did not think to check if it was actually going with the prevailing wind though I do remember there being only a light wind that day). It did not radically change shapes or take on any definite shapes but just stayed generally oblong (like the "parachute" story). The sky was clear and it was around sunset so the object was fairly well lit. However, I had a hard time focusing on it. Sound-wise I heard nothing from it and the neighborhood was quiet. It was about the size of my fingernail at arm's length. Moved right to left about a fist-width every second or so. I watched it for about ten seconds then it became obscured behind the tree branches so I walked down the block about 40 feet to a clear view. But in the process, I looked down for a second, and when I got to the clearing, I could not find the object again. Very puzzling.

Blue Lights in Neillsville
Occurred: 1/12/2004 18:30
Entered as 01/12/2004 18:30
Reported 2/5/2004 7:31:34 am 07:31
Posted (NUFORC) 2/122004
Location: Neillsville, Wis.
Duration: 5 minutes red-yellow-blue lights in the southern-western sky in Neillsville, Wis.

"This sighting occurred on a clear night; no lights from the city since the city is to the north and sighting was to the south-south western sky. Craft shape was hard to discern. The craft had lights red-blue-yellow which flashed and had white lights on the edges of the craft. The craft was at an altitude of approximately 500-600 feet above the ground at a distance of approximately 1 to 2 miles, I think. It is hard to judge distance. There were no sounds that I could hear. There was no wind. Air temperature was approximately 20 degrees F. There were stars out. The craft apparently was hovering since it was not moving in any direction. My two dogs were very restless and were angrily growling toward the same direction as the craft. I watched the craft for about 3-5 minutes trying to see a shape or rule out other explanations such as aircraft or a star or planet. However, there was no movement, no sounds, and the lights did not strobe like that of an aircraft. There was no vapor trail that I could see. I went into the house to get the camcorder to zoom in on the craft and film it. I was in the house for approximately five minutes. When I returned, the craft was gone. I have not seen it since; however, a neighbor approximately 1.5 miles away did see it."

2005 UFO EVENTS

Green Bay Packers football player Aaron Rodgers sees a UFO in New Jersey in February 2005: Rodgers said it was just like that movie "Independence Day."

"It was a large orange, left-to-right-moving object," Rodgers said. "Because of the overcast nature of the night and the snow, you couldn't make out... It was behind kind of the clouds we were seeing, but it was definitively large in the night sky, moving from left to right."

"And it goes out of sight and we look at each other and go, 'What in the f--- was that?'"

(Philadelphia *Inquirer*)

Space Station UFO

In 2005, astronaut Leroy Chiao was commander of the International Space Station for six and a half months. During a spacewalk with cosmonaut Salizhan Sharipov, the two were installing navigation antennas. They were 230 miles above Earth, traveling at over 17,000 miles per hour when something unusual caught Chiao's eye.

"I saw some lights that seemed to be in a line and it

was almost like an upside-down check mark, and I saw them fly by and thought it was awfully strange," Chiao told *The Huffington Post*.

Also in 2005

Stanton T. Friedman publishes *Top Secret/Majic*, an account of the UFO crash and coverup at Roswell, New Mexico.

Local Sightings

A Sylvan Ridge Native

This was fall, 1966. We were at our farm near Sylvan. It was 4 am. I got up and saw this big orange ball in the sky. It was in the northwest sky. It was too early for the Sun. I learned later that a neighbor also saw it.

A Man from La Crosse

(from UFO Wisconsin) "At about 7:15 on Tuesday, Oct. 4 2005 I walked out my front door which faces west and immediately saw what I first thought to be the evening star (which is it Mercury or Venus?), but I realized it wasn't it was too far to the south and it looked just like the star of Bethlehem. It had a large very bright main body with what looked like small points on the side and a long bright tail below. I called to my wife to have her look so I was for sure I wasn't seeing things or my eyes were deceiving me. She saw what I saw. We looked at the object in my binoculars and it looked like an upside-down crescent moon with fingers, legs, things below, it's hard to describe. The things below made up the tail. It was moving but was very slow slower it seemed than the setting stars. Kath watched for about twenty mins I watched for a while longer. The object moved in a south-westerly direction and eventually passed behind some clouds at which time we noticed that the clouds began to illuminate from the object. It then vanished behind the clouds. That's it I asked a few other people but no one saw it. I am an avid skywatcher and look up each and every time I go outside day or night. So, I know when something is not normal and this was not normal. Whether it was an aberration of the atmosphere or some-thing else it was exciting and I am glad I have a witness to coordinate what I saw.

Door County UFO

(from UFO Wisconsin) "It was our second night at campsite 10 at Newport State Park. My wife and I were camping with our friends. At about 3:15 am, which would have been Saturday the 13th of August, one of our dogs was whining to go out. After he diligently took care of business, I let him back into the tent and walked out onto the beach to observe the meteor shower. Though it had been clear earlier that night and the night before we had been disappointed in the lack of meteors seen. The sky was clear as could be and I looked to the northeast, scanning the sky for falling stars.

"Before long I noticed a single white light above the tree line. It was quite a distance away. At first, I thought it was a planet until I noticed it moving in a clockwise circle. I took note that none of the other stars in the sky were moving, so I figured the wind was moving the tops of the trees to give this star the appearance of motion. I walked back about fifteen feet, making certain that from my vantage point there was no way the trees could interfere with my view. Still, the light continued its clockwise circling. After a couple of minutes, it broke into three lights, as if forming the points of an equilateral triangle. Then the three lights continued in the clockwise circling. This lasted for several more minutes until they finally converged back into one point and quickly faded off to the northeast.

"Of course, a couple of times I was tempted to go wake my wife and my friends, but I figured the minute I did the object would disappear. Instead, I thought it best to observe the light as long as I could and let them sleep.

"I have no idea if this was a phenomenon or some intelligence. I had no feeling of any presence and I felt more curious than anything. Besides, I know what I saw, the circling lights over Lake Michigan."

A Man from Keshena

(from UFO Wisconsin) "I have a cabin in Keshena, Wisconsin right on Legend Lake. I view the stars nightly from my deck overlooking the lake. Almost nightly I see ODD things in the sky, UFOs, (unidentified flying objects) flying in patterns, sometimes flying alone across the sky. On September 6, 2005, in the Western Sky VERY FAR AWAY, if you were looking directly west and by using your watch for a direction, at the 2:00 area in the sky, a BRIGHT White Star appeared suddenly, out of NO WHERE, a short time after it stopped bright Red, Orange and Blue lights (objects) began going around the Bright Star, this lasted about 1/2 hour. My wife and I got a pair of binoculars and were looking at the star with binoculars, the objects that were colored and were circulating seemed to be rectangular in shape. There were 3 of these objects going around and around the STAR, then another bright white object came from the North-Eastern direction and suddenly STOPPED near the Star with the rotating objects. The colored objects seemed to go behind the Bright star at this time and were not visible any longer. A bright RED object came from the bright star that came from the Northeastern direction and SHOT towards the Star that had the 3 colored objects rotating it. The Red object began circulating the other star, all of a sudden, the bright Star I first viewed SHOT out and away into the sky and disappeared, the Red object returned to the Bright White Object (UFO) that it came from and seemed to disappear into the White Star. The Bright White Star (UFO) then SHOT back out towards the direction it came from and then just disappeared in the dark, star-filled sky. This viewing lasted about 2 hours total. Some of my neighbors were viewing this beautiful encounter along with my wife and myself. The neighbors were talking about it with their visitors that were sitting by the campfire during this sighting. I see things like this in the North, Western, Northwestern, Northeastern sky almost nightly when I am up there viewing the stars from my deck overlooking the Lake."

Top UFO Counties in Wisconsin
(from Filer's Files)
1. Walworth (39 reports)
2. Pierce (37)
3. Douglas (33)
4. Polk (33)
5. Door (32)

6. Eau Claire (25)
7. Shawano (22)
8. Pepin (22)
9. Grant (19)
10. Fond du Lac (19)
11. Barron (14)
12. Langlade (12)
13. Price (12)

2006 UFO EVENTS

The Chicago O'Hare UFO sighting: On November 14, 2006, a UFO was spotted over O'Hare Airport in Chicago which is widely considered to have been one of the most dramatic UFO sightings in years. Just before sundown, a large disc-shaped object was seen hovering over one of the gates of the airport, and then it suddenly flew straight up in the air, leaving a hole straight up in the clouds where it had passed through. The disc was seen by numerous airline employees and passengers. This event was reported widely in the press, including the *Associated Press*, the *Chicago Tribune*, *USA Today*, and a host of others. A few months later, actor and UFO buff Dan Ackroyd revealed that he had acquired photos and even video of the sighting and was planning to use them in an upcoming documentary film.

Local Sightings

A Woman from Viroqua
We were at the home of a relative on a ridge near

Viola. We were sitting on the deck just after sundown. It was in July of this year.

Off to the right was a large, circular, bright light almost as big as the Moon. It was about the color of a star. It was not really high up in the sky, although it was higher than the tops of the trees. It appeared and disappeared.

That night, about half an hour later, again in the east, at about the same place, there appeared another light. This one was smaller, but it was still bigger than a star. It moved from north to south. Then it stopped where the other light had appeared. Then this light went straight up in the air and disappeared. Five of us saw this.

A Man from Viola

I was going down State Highway 56 and turned onto County Highway G. Just there in the valley was this thing hovering in the valley. It had wings and was oblong—underneath was a basket-type thing. There were two bright lights on the wing thing. Two of us saw it. It went up the valley, heading to the east, and sort of disappeared. We took County High-way G to the top of the hill and again we saw it in the sky. We watched it go off into the northern sky. It never got very high.

A Non-UFO-related Mystery—a Woman from Viroqua.

Friends of mine were traveling down State Highway 27 near Rising Sun. Just as they passed the cemetery of the church, a strange animal came running out of the woods. It looked like a combination of a bear and a cow. It crossed the cemetery and jumped over the fence and went out into the road in front of their car. It jumped and then landed in the ditch below the road. When they looked for it, it had completely vanished.

Another Cow-like Mystery

Viroqua author Jay Rath, in the *W-Files*, tells a UFO story involving a cow-like creature:

"At about 10:30 pm. on December 2, 1974, near Frederic in Polk County, William Bosak, a 69-year-old dairy farmer, was driving home when he saw a disc-shaped craft beside the road. 'I can remember it just as if it were yesterday,' Bosak told me.

"The lower half of the craft was shrouded in mist. It had a curved glass window, and inside the brightly lit compartment, Bosak saw a creature covered with dark tan fur, except for its face and chin.

"'He was looking out the window and it was a different kind of character than you'd see on this Earth,' he said.

"'It looked a good deal like a man but it had a different-looking face than you'd see. It had a kind of cow-looking face.'

"Asked to elaborate, Bosak explained that the face had hair on its sides. The ears stuck out from the head about three inches and the eyes were large and protruding.

"'The creature held its arms above its head, and its expression led Bosak to believe that 'it was just as scared as I was'.

"After about 10 seconds, Bosak quickly drove away, and as he did so, his car lights dimmed, the engine sounded as if it were missing and he heard a soft whooshing noise.

"The next day Bosak returned to the area and found a

round spot, 6 feet in diameter pressed down into the hayfield" (pgs. 14-15)

2007 UFO EVENTS

Reports and photographs begin to circulate in central California and near Lake Tahoe of small hovering craft in the skies. The photographs released did not at all resemble the classic UFO disc. Some speculated that they may have been military aerial drones or UAVs (unmanned aerial vehicles) such as have been used in Afghanistan and Iraq.

Two important books about the Roswell incident, which this year celebrated its 60th anniversary. One was by the son of the Air Force officer who first investigated the alleged UFO crash, Col. Jesse Marcel. Jesse Marcel, Jr. has written *The Roswell Legacy*. Another one: *Witness to Roswell*, has various Wisconsin connections. An anonymous southwestern Wisconsin Roswell researcher says that he provided two important leads in the book, which was itself co-written by Wisconsin native Donald R. Schmitt and Tom Carey. One of these leads was the identity of the famed missing nurse of the story—who it turns out was the late Rosemary McManus, also of Wisconsin.

Local Sightings

A Woman from Viola

I have had 2 UFO experiences that seem to really stick in my mind.

The first being just south of Lansing, IA near the power plant. I was only about 10 years old. It was a really cold winter night. My dad had told my older sister and me to get the dog some extra straw for her dog house. We raced with her taking the long way around the driveway, and I taking the shorter route, walking, balancing myself across a 4x4 beam. I was carrying a flashlight so as to see the beam well enough. I had made it about 1/2 way across when all a sudden there was what seemed like a huge ball of light coming down into the valley at an incredible rate of speed! It came down, then without any sound, went straight up and out of sight over the next hill. I was absolutely terrified. I crawled and bawled all the way to the barn which was about 40 or so yards away. My sister had beaten me to the barn and was unaware of anything happening. She couldn't understand why I was so scared. I tried to explain but she made fun of me. In fact, when I tried to tell the rest of my family, they made fun of me also. *Oh well, at least I believe...*

The 2nd encounter I had was when I was 19 living on Salem Ridge near La Farge, WI. My husband at the time was injured and unable to do chores. So, I was in process of feeding the cows silage from the back of our ol' 66 Chev pickup. I was standing in the bed of the truck and looking occasionally upward admiring the fall sky with all its dazzling stars.

While gazing, I noticed 3 bright red blinking lights off

in the distance. They appeared to move closer to me. I also noticed that the lights formed a triangular pattern, pulsing and moving very very close. What was really odd is that as the lights neared, I could hear no sound and could see no outline or possibly a plane or helicopter. The lights were so close, they were nearing treetop level. It was then that I decided to jump out of the back of the truck and hide under it. The "lights" hovered above with no sound for what seemed like possibly 5 minutes or so and disappeared again into the night. Now, THAT scared me a lot even as an adult. I still think about that every time I'm outside at night. It gives me a chill.

A report from UFO Casebook website, from Shiocton, Wisconsin:

"06-07-Friday evening almost 9:00 pm CST I was out cleaning my pool. I had looked into the sky as it was just getting dark, stormy, and very cloudy. Jay, a friend of mine and my sister's, was with me. Suddenly I saw out of the corner of my eye a very bright light come out of nowhere.

"I thought it was the planet Venus. I told Jay to look at that and pointed to the area of the sky where I saw the star. Jay looked up and as he did this object shot to the right, then straight up and right back where it was in a split second. 'Did you see that?' he said. I replied, 'Oh yes, that was awesome.'

"We called the girls over and told them what we had seen. They looked up 'Yeah, so? A star.' Then they started laughing, cracking jokes at us. About the time they were getting their kicks, the object started moving again. 'Not so funny now, is it?' I asked...

"I snapped off 12-15 pics. All of these pictures I saw on the screen before I snapped the pictures...None of the photos looked anything like what we saw when shooting the pictures. Some of the photos have been enlarged to give a better viewing of the photos."

A Woman from Readstown

"This was on September 13, 1994. I was driving on Hwy 130 between Dodgeville and Lone Rock. That takes you to Highway 14. My sister was following behind me. What I saw was a light. It was flashing and had many changing colors. More so than any airplane. The shape was like a straight line like it was a sphere. I know it wasn't an airplane. It didn't have a distinct shape plus it had too many colors plus it stayed to the right of me the whole trip. This went on for twenty-five or thirty minutes, the whole time it took us to drive to Readstown. If we had had cellphones then we would have been calling each other up and talking about it. When we drove into Readstown on Highway 14 from the Richland Center side, the light just took off and flew out over the valley and up into the sky and disappeared. The minute my sister and I got out of our cars we both ran up to each other saying: 'Did you see that?!'"

Occurred: 9/1/2007 19:00 (Entered as : 9/1/07 19:00)
Reported: 9/5/2007 12:06:28 pm 12:06
Posted: 10/8/2007
Location: Dodgeville and Oconomowoc, WI
Shape: Disk
Duration: first 1 minute and second
Two Alien Space Crafts over Dodgeville and Oconomowoc

We were driving in the car through Dodgeville, when I spotted a silver disk flying east. It would disappear and then reappear and flew up and down. It emitted a goldish color. It looked like a disk except the top was pushed up. It was right across from the Culvers on the east side of the road. Then it suddenly vanished. About an hour and thirty-five minutes later when we were in Oconomowoc it with another craft flew out of the sky. They changed color from gold to yellow to red to orange and finally to a silver color. They looked like the one in Dodgeville and were flying in the same direction. It left a blueish purple haze after it. Then shot straight up like a rocket and vanished. I personally do not believe in UFOs but this is very real. And life-like.

Occurred: 9/8/2007 20:45 (Entered as : 09/08/2007 20:45)
Reported: 9/8/2007 6:58:33 pm 18:58
Posted: 10/8/2007
Location: Onalaska, WI
Shape: Circle
Duration:10 minutes
Round dimly lit object moves and appears to notice the observer.

As I got out of my car upon returning home from work, I looked up into the sky to see a dimly lit, round object high up above my home. It appeared to be illuminated underneath and was a dim red color barely noticeable but it could still be picked out in the light cloud cover it moved into. It moved from North West to the South East at a high rate of speed and then began to slow somewhat. My outdoor floodlight, which is on a motion sensor, went off illuminating me in the backyard, and I then saw the object slow down and hover for about five minutes. My flood lamp timed out and shut off and I then watched the object move off to the South West. It was almost as if the thing was watching me watching it because it did not stop and hover until my floodlight went off.

2008 UFO EVENTS

The biggest UFO story of the year was the series of sightings of enormous UFOs over the skies of Stephenville, Texas. The fact that solid, reputable people, including pilots and law officers were seeing a low flying object almost big enough to cover the sky is in itself interesting. But the fact that all of this is happening a short distance away from the summer residence of president George W. Bush makes the story intriguing.

The UFO was witnessed by about thirty residents of this town, which calls itself the dairy capital of Texas (and where now on sale are T-shirts featuring a Holstein cow being beamed into a UFO). From the ABC news website:

> "Steve Allen, a 50-year-old pilot, was at a campfire with friends and says the object was a mile long and half a mile wide. 'I don't know if it was a biblical experience or somebody from a different universe or whatever but it was definitely not from around these parts,' Allen said.
>
> "Allen drew a sketch of the object, which he said

traveled at amazing speed without making a sound. While drawing, Allen told Von Fremd that he saw 'an arch shape converted in a vertical shape, and then it split and made two of them, and then these turned into just fire and it was gone.'

"In October of 2008, the British military issued a second batch of files it has accumulated on UFOs. An earlier release had taken place in the spring of this year. The latest release consisted of 1,500 pages of documents which debunked a number of cases, but left unexplained a report of a pilot of a military jet ordered to shoot at a UFO, only to have it immediately vanish, and a couple of cases of close calls at airports with UFOs nearly hitting airliners only to also vanish."

Local Sightings

On July 31 of this year strange objects swept over the sky in various places in Wisconsin and other states with LaFarge being one of the sites that reported the sightings. An anonymous correspondent from LaFarge posted this on the National UFO Reporting Center, with the time of the sighting being 9:20 pm.

Occurred: 7/31/2008 21:20 (Entered as : 7/31/08 21:20)
Reported: 8/1/2008 11:32:10 am 11:32
Posted: 8/12/2008
Location: La Farge, WI
Shape and Duration: few minutes series of red lights appear-merge and dissipate-La Farge, WI

Unidentified object reporting: La Farge, Wisconsin Thursday, July 31, 2008 at dusk 6 adults and two children were coming home after a dinner outing. As we live in the country, we have a beautiful night sky. We often star gaze and get out our telescope to observe... Upon getting out of our vehicles, I noticed a light shining through a very large pine tree that is in our yard. I recognized that it was peculiarly large and so I walked over to look at it. I walked around the tree to observe the light and realized I wasn't looking at an airplane or helicopter. There were approximately 8-12 large red lights in a perfect horizontal line, just above the tree line. We live on a ridge top so I had almost a 360-degree panoramic view of the sky.

I did not notice a body of the aircraft, however but couldn't stop saying "oh my goodness, you guys come look at this." Everyone was busy unloading stuff out of the car and it felt like I was talking to myself. My daughter, 8, came next to me and said, "Mama, what is that?" There was another line of approximately 5 to 6 lights to the left of the larger set of lights, which were at almost a 35-degree angle.

At the very moment I finally said, "oh my goodness, it is a UFO," while pretty much jumping up and down in disbelief, the two streams of lights merged together into one and completely disappeared into thin air. There was no turning around, no smoke from a jet, no noise at all. I said, "Did anyone see that, did anyone see that?" My sister-in-law said she saw the very end of the lights merge together and disappear. Now, it was dusk and light enough for me to see a body of whatever it was that I saw, but I did not see that. However, when we went into the house, I asked my daughter to draw what she saw. She is incredibly gifted with art, and has definitely never been exposed to talk of nor seen any movies with UFOs. She had no preconceived perception of what a

UFO is... She drew exactly what I saw with oblong shapes around the lights. I don't know why she saw a body around the lights, but she did. It sounds absolutely crazy, but I think children can sometimes connect with what adults cannot. Perhaps I was so numb from the lights that I couldn't comprehend the body of an aircraft type object. I don't know.

Stranger yet, I called the police department because I wanted to know if anyone else had sighted this. They said no and just as I was hanging up the telephone, two US Army jets hovered over the area where I saw the unidentified objects. It was obvious they were looking for something. When they couldn't or didn't see what perhaps appeared on radar (I don't know how they would know this was there and where it was, etc.) they turned their jets around and faced our home.

For a moment, I tried to tell myself this was what I previously saw, however it was much different. The lights I saw in perspective to being on the ground and standing, where comparable to the size of car headlights. This is how large they were in the sky. On top of that, when the jets left, they were extremely loud. It is very clear when jets hover...the object I saw did not make a single sound. It disappeared into thin air—in a matter of a second or so it was completely gone.

I froze, and cried, in disbelief with my daughter at my side. My family was relatively upset they didn't get to see what I saw. My sister-in-law was pretty frightened, and said, "I am going to pretend I didn't' see what I just saw." I said, "I hope this is just the beginning." My daughter said, "Mama, what is a UFO?" My story may be crazy, seem unreal, I don't know what it sounds like. I have never researched UFOs but I tell you, once it got into my brain, I tried every way possible to discredit what I saw, and I know that is EXACTLY what I saw.

However, five minutes earlier, at 9:15 pm, in Grand Marsh, Wisconsin, in Adams County, a very similar thing was spotted and also reported to the same website:

Occurred: 7/31/2008 21:15 (Entered as 7/31/08 21:15)
Reported: 8/1/2008 10:20:20 am 10:20
Posted: 8/12/2008
Location: Grand Marsh, WI
Shape: Formation
Duration: Four spheres of light arranged in straight line.

I was driving north of Grand Marsh, WI on 6th Ave. just after dusk. There were no clouds in the sky and it was still too bright for there to be many stars out. The area that I was driving through is all farm fields and forest.

In the distance above the horizon on the west side of the road I saw four spheres of white light that were arranged in a straight line. The spheres were quite bright, packed closely together but just enough space between that you could distinguish each sphere. I was looking at the lights for a couple of seconds and they just disappeared.

About 2 minutes later I saw the spheres of light again. This time I actually saw the four balls of light suddenly appear in the horizon on the east side of the road. They appeared slightly larger (closer) this time, again arranged in a straight line, although the angle of the line was in the opposite direction that it was previously. The spheres were there for 3-4 seconds and then disappeared again.

I saw no other cars the whole time that I was on this particular road and don't remember any other lights that would have caused any reflections on the windshield.

And cited as 9:20 pm, same time as the LaFarge sighting, came this report to the same website from Almond, Wisconsin, near Steven Point:

Occurred: 7/31/2008 21:20 (Entered as 07/31/08 21:20)
Reported: 8/1/2008 11:48:49 am 11:48
Posted: 8/12/2008
Location: Almond, WI
Shape: Triangle
Duration:30 seconds V shaped winking lights.
As I was driving home last night, at about 9:20 pm, I noticed a strange string of lights near the horizon. I live near Oshkosh Wi, so I thought maybe it was a plane heading over to EAA. But then the lights started to wink on and off, in sort of a V shape. It looked really large too.
It lasted just a few seconds and then was gone! There were about 4 or 5 evenly spaced lights in sort of a V pattern, that got closer together each time they blinked, until they disappeared.
This happened right over a small town in Wisconsin called Bancroft. It is in Portage County.

Two minutes later, this was spotted near Portage, Wis, from the same website:

Occurred: 7/31/2008 21:22 (Entered as : 07/31/08 21:22)
Reported: 7/31/2008 9:30:13 pm 21:30
Posted: 8/12/2008

Location: Portage, WI
Shape: Formation
Duration:15 Minutes UFO's spotted in Central WI. Line of lights.

I was driving home from Madison back up to the Stevens Point area on a Thursday night. We witnessed bright, white lights in the western sky just north of Portage, WI. The lights varied. A single light would appear, and sometimes multiply into many separate lights. At times there were as many as 5 all in a horizontal, straight line. The lights would stay in place for a few moments and then disappear, only to appear a few minutes later. At one point there were two lights that turned into two separate lines of 6 lights in total. The lights were brighter and larger than stars, but appeared lower than stars in the sky, yet higher than fireworks would appear.

The entire time, the lights expanded westward and horizontally. Even though we were traveling 70 mph in a car, the lights remained in the same part of the sky.

After 15 minutes of seeing these lights appear, disappear, and repeat, they finally stopped.

And finally, at Omro and Mosinee both at 9:30 pm, are these reports:

Occurred: 7/31/2008 21:30 (Entered as 07/31/08 21:30)
Reported: 8/1/2008 8:03:44 pm 20:03
Posted: 8/12/2008
Location: Omro (northwest of), WI
Shape: Light
Duration: 5 minutes Sequence of bright white stationary

lights appearing and disappearing, all in a horizontal row.

Last night (July 31, 2008) around 9:30 pm CST, my husband and I witnessed very bright white lights in the distance 'appear' and then 'disappear' several times. These lights did not move at all.

First one—"on", then "off". (a minute or two pass) Next one "on", another "on", then both "off". (a minute or two passed as we stare into the night sky above the tree line) Next one "on", two "on", three "on" (all in a horizontal row evenly spaced) and then all "off". (a minute or two pass) Then, as I head into the house to get away from the mosquitos (!!), my husband says "one—two..." so I quickly look back and see one-by-one, four more bright lights turn "on" (closer together than before and more to the left, but still in a straight horizontal line). The six lights turned "on" in sequence from right to left, and all at once, disappeared.

That was the end of our show for the night, but it reminded us of an evening a few years back. We had seen a similar show, but much closer and much brighter. That night, they reminded me of the rectangle-shape of those bright lights at football games. But these were across the river from us and much higher than any lights would be. Our lights in the house flickered and my phone died while in the middle of telling my mom what we had seen, so I'd had to call her back. It was a similar sequence of light turning 'on' in a row, and then all at once, disappearing. If you weren't looking right then, you'd easily miss it, because they were only lit for about 10 seconds or so.

We never expected to see anything like this again! Our background: interest in space, like watching NOVA, but that's about it. Never imagined we'd see something like this—feel like we can't tell anyone, or they'll think we're crazy!"

Mosinee
Occurred: 7/31/2008 21:30 (Entered as 07/31/08 21:30)
Reported: 7/31/2008 10:19:07 pm 22:19
Posted: 8/12/2008
Location: Mosinee, WI
Shape: Light
Duration: 15-20 seconds 5 lights in straight horizontal line that faded out—no noise heard

My Mom and I saw something very weird on our walk. At around 9:15 pm on July 31st 2008 over Mosinee, Wisconsin I witnessed a straight horizontal line of 5 yellowish lights. The tops of the perfectly round lights seemed to have a little bit of red in them too. They were kind of weak in intensity and just above the tree tops over a potato field about 2 blocks away. I only saw them for about 5 seconds before I grabbed my Mom's arm to look at them too. As I did that they quickly started to fade out one light at a time from the right to left. She saw that last light sparkling before it disappeared.

We continued on our walk for about 15 minutes and came to a spot where we could see the sky in full view over the potato field. We stopped and looked up towards the south to see if we saw something to explain it. We watched for about 3 minutes. Then all of a sudden to the SW we saw it again, but this time it was really bright and lasted for about 15-20 seconds. And it faded out from right to left again, but faster this time.

It never appeared to be "flying" or moving, just

hovered there. It was as high up as a helicopter would fly and about a quarter mile away from us. There was nothing in the path of our view, completely open and clear skies. It was unbelievable!!! We are really interested to see if anyone else saw the same thing. We can't explain it—like nothing we had EVER seen.

Similar lights were reported on the same night, within an hour or so of the same time in Yuma and Wellton, Arizona, Salisbury, North Carolina, and Chesterfield and Russellville Arkansas. All of these sightings were reported to the same website: NUFORC.com.

2009 UFO EVENTS

The wife of the Prime Minister of Japan published a book that says she was abducted by ETs and rode on a spaceship to Venus. Her husband says it was a dream. Because of his large eyes, he has long been jokingly called "the alien."

After sixty years of study, the British Ministry of Defense closed down its "UFO desk". They stated that the files were simply collected and were not uncovering any real threats to Britain. UFO author Nick Pope was at one time involved in this effort.

Former NASA astronaut Edgar Mitchell said at a speech on Earth Day at the National Press Club that there is no doubt that Earth is being visited by ETs from other planets. Mitchell, who is a native of UFO hot spot Roswell, New Mexico, says he was told this information by a high-ranking US Navy Admiral.

Local Sightings

A Woman from Readstown

In summer, about 1963 or 1964, I was in a truck with my father-in-law, coming back from the feed mill in Gays Mills, heading toward our farm. He was driving. It must have been about 3:30 pm or 4 pm. We were at the top of a hill about to go down into the valley where our farm was. Suddenly, he said: "It is sure getting dark." And then the truck motor killed and we stopped dead on the gravel road. We looked above us and saw an enormous object above us. It was just over the treetops. It stretched from where we were to being over the barn in our valley. That made it about half a mile long. It was about two stories tall. There were windows above that had changing lights. There were beams of light coming down out of the craft and hitting our barn.

It made no noise, although you could feel a sort of pulsation. I remember feeling the pulsation on the metal dashboard of the pick-up truck. My father-in-law got out of the truck and looked in amazement at it. "What in the f--- is that?" he said. I don't remember how long we looked at it, maybe five minutes. After a bit, the beams of light stopped hitting our barn. Then the object raised up a bit and shot off to the northwest, disappearing in just a few seconds.

My father-in-law said, "Don't say anything about this to anybody or they will think we are nuts." I never did, and he never did either. I never even told my husband.

About three weeks after that thing was there, our cows started throwing calves. We called our Vet and he called in the State Vet, they concluded that the feed we were giving the animals had absolutely no vitamins, minerals, or anything. But we grew it right on our farm, and the feed before was always okay, and the feed afterward was always okay. It was just the feed, including the corn and the silage, that was in the barn when that thing was overhead that day that was not good. That never happened before and it never happened again. Forty-four cows lost their calves. We had to give the cows vitamin A, D, and E until they became pregnant again and we got new feed.

A year and a half later, my father-in-law got throat cancer and he had to take radiation treatments in La Crosse. He would come home quite sick, and on one of these times coming home he suddenly brought up our seeing the object in the sky. He said: "I'm not crazy and I know that you aren't crazy. And we know what we saw!" He added that he had also seen something like that years earlier when he was a young boy. He had never told that to anybody before, he told me.

From National UFO Reporting Center:

Occurred: 7/25/2009 21:40 (Entered as 07/25/09 21:40)
Reported: 7/28/2009 4:20:23 pm 16:20
Posted: 8/5/2009
Location: Cashton, WI
Shape: Oval
Duration: 15 minutes. 3 lights coming from the north to southeast. 2 red, 1 white. Total time 15 minutes. All separate sightings.

I called the hotline to report this today 7/28/09.

Saturday night July 25th around 9:40 pm CDT my

husband and I were driving to our house on a ridge top in western Wisconsin. I noticed to the north a light that was heading southeast. This light was white. I watched it for a few seconds and then remarked to my husband, "look at the light, but it does not appear to be a plane, it has no blinking lights". The light was lower than a satellite...but because it was way in front of me it appeared to be airplane height. The light went off to the east and disappeared.

We drove into our driveway got out of the car, my husband went into the house to let the dogs out and I stood there. I looked up and from the north came a red light toward me. I called to my husband "look". We both watched the light approach us, it appeared to be low, and it was red, round, not blinking and no sound. Its size was bigger than a star... medical helicopter size. We watched for 15 seconds or so as it headed in a southeast direction.

I started to walk the dogs to the north looked up and there was another light. I called to my husband "it's back." It came from the north, red, low, round, no sound, not blinking...flying steady. It headed in a southeast direction above me. Same dimensions as the first light... really identical. Both sightings from the house were just a few minutes apart.
((NUFORC Note: ISS. PD))

UFO Footage Broadcast by Channel 8-La Crosse

On March 11, 2009, Channel 8 broadcast some clips from an 11-minute-long video of a UFO filmed by a man from Sparta:

"A circular shape floating in the air. I have no idea what the f--- that is!"

Most of the tape consists of the reactions of two men, one of them holding the camera. One of them has apparently had a previous UFO experience and compares the round object hovering in the air to one he saw previously. They compare the object to things such as planes, helicopters, and rockets with some degree of familiarity with them: "That ain't no Roman candle shot off at Fort McCoy!" A woman comes on the soundtrack for a while expressing her skepticism about the whole thing. The object can be seen to change colors on the screen. At the end of one of them says, "They are preparing an invasion." The other responds, "I wouldn't doubt it."

It turns out that the two men are father and son: Zach and his father, Paul Rueckheim, of rural Sparta. They filmed the object on their farm. Channel 8 showed it to Gordon Stewart, director of the UW-La Crosse Planetarium. "I don't think it's a meteor, I don't think it's a comet. No comet I've ever seen behaves like that. I don't think it's a satellite because a satellite would move regularly. I could suspect first by its behavior of being a weather balloon." They consulted with the La Crosse weather bureau and they said that although they do release weather balloons it was unlikely to be one of theirs.

From National UFO Reporting Service website
Occurred : 11/1/2008 20:00 (Entered as : 11/01/08 20:00)
Reported: 4/5/2009 7:42:18 pm 19:42
Posted: 4/14/2009
Location: HWY 21 (Monroe County), WI
Shape: Light
Duration:5 seconds Light was there then off like a switch

"My wife was driving west on highway 21 in Wisconsin to visit her parents the night before Thanksgiving and I was in the passenger seat bored out of my mind and we just passed a four-way stop on the highway when from the right corner of my eye I noticed a fast-moving yellowish light kind of more like a car light yellow in the sky and I started to point to it and say to my wife "Look at that pla—" by the time I tried to say "plane" it was like someone hit a switch and turned off the lights and there was nothing. My wife did see it in time. I originally thought it was just a military jet hauling ass but there were no other red or green lights of that sort.

2010 UFO EVENTS

Perhaps the most spectacular UFO sighting of the past 12 months occurred in December in northern Norway. A bizarre blue spiral was reported and photographed in the dark winter sky. Various Norwegian experts were of the opinion that it was a failed Russian missile test. However, the Russian government denied that they were doing any missile tests at that time in the region in question—the White Sea. See: http://www.dailymail.co.uk/news/worldnews/article-1234430/Mystery-spiral-blue-light-display-hovers-Norway.html

Meanwhile, some governments appeared to be taking quiet but significant actions regarding the UFO subject. The British government continued to release UFO files and the result was the exposure of a couple of encounters between military aircraft and UFOs. British UFO files were posted online at http://www.nationalarchives.gov.uk/ufos/.

The United Nations also appointed an official to be the point of contact for any possible Star Nations. Dr. Mazlan Othman of Malaysia has been the head of the

United Nations Office for Outer Space Affairs (UNoosa). In September the UN Appointed her to fill the role of greeter should alien visitors arrive. She was appointed to UNoosa by the Secretary-General in 1999 and she has been instrumental in the training of the Malaysian space program.

China was the scene of a UFO forcing airports to close on two occasions—in July and September. In July, the airport at Xiaoshan was closed by aircraft controllers because an unidentified flying object was hovering over the airport. Flights had to be diverted. The same thing happened in September at the Baotou airport in China's Inner Mongolia province. No official explanation was offered for either incident.

Journalist Leslie Kean attracted a good deal of mainstream press with the publication of her book *UFOs: Generals, Pilots and Government Officials Go on the Record.*

On Oct. 13, UFOs were spotted over New York City, Russia, and Malaysia, attracting a good deal of press attention.

Local Sightings

A Man and Woman from Viroqua

The man: This happened in the late 1960s on our farm west of Viroqua. It was in the middle of the night. All of a sudden, I woke up and there was a loud humming outside. We slept upstairs; my parents slept downstairs.

The woman: It was one of those nights when it was really hot and still. I got out of bed because the fan quit and all the current quit.

The man: We looked at it from the upstairs window—out in the fields. Later on, there was a 30 ft. space across the area where crops did not grow for a year or two. There was no craft, there was just a big white light.

The woman: All you could see was this big, white light. Even the trees were white. And there was this high-pitched hum which was like what you get when an airplane is just taking off.

The man: It was a loud hum like just before you are ready to take off in a plane.

The woman: Neighbors a mile away told us the next day they saw the light.

The man: My folks saw it too, but they are both dead.

The woman: I talked with my mother-in-law about that night, so it wasn't a dream. There is a big power line that goes near our house. The next day men from the electric company were up at the transformer fixing something that was burned up.

A Woman from Readstown (taking place in the 1960s)
    "I remember that it was really bright and scary. I think that I was around 10 so I would have been in 4th grade and Mike in 5th. We had been sledding on a very cold day. I remember that no one else wanted to go with us because it was so cold. It was before supper but

getting dark. We were walking back up the hill and this flying light appeared in front of us but not close to us. We were about halfway up the hill and it was at the top. We just stood there and watched it hover. We were not sure what we were seeing or if we were really seeing anything. I remember Mike and I running faster than we had ever run before down the hill to the school gym door pulling our sleds behind us. The gym door was locked. We just stood there watching the light for I'm not sure how long. It landed or came really close to landing and hovered. I do not remember seeing any legs or wheels. It was horizontally oval but so bright that it was hard to see anything except the brightness. We did not hear any noise. We did not see an alien or anything like that. When it just stayed there, we took off and ran as fast as we could to a local cafe. No one believed us but I did get my dad to drive up there. The object and light were gone. The next day my dad and I found a huge circle of melted snow just on the other side of the fence. There were no footprints anywhere. It snowed a lot that next day (It must have been a Friday night because we didn't go to school the next day.) Everyone just thought that we had made all this up because no one else saw anything. I remember the restaurant customers joking and asking me if I had seen any more flying saucers or met any little green men.

"I do know that we were afraid but that we never felt threatened that it was after us or that it would hurt us. It was not that type of fear. If it was, I could probably remember more details!

"I wish that Mike or my parents were still alive because then maybe we could pick each other's brains for more details for you. After 30+ years I do not remember details. My best memory is that we knew what we had seen and no one believed us!"

From MUFON reports of Wisconsin

(posted July 7, 2010)

"It's an old story of mine. Happened to me when I was working for the summer as a student in Wisconsin Dells, WI area in the summer of 2003. Event happened in early calendar summer at night (around midnight) on some night of probably late July or maybe early August. Night was kind of bright thanks to a bright full moon.

"At late night (probably before midnight) I wanted to get some fresh air and decided to have a lonely ride in my car. I took my car from home (we were living between Lake Delton and Wisconsin Dells) and traveled at night through Broadway (in Wisconsin Dells), then leaving Wisconsin Dells downtown area behind and taking right turn on some highway (from google maps I think it was Route 16).

"I have traveled a couple miles East and then pulled over to small local dirt road (on left) ending in the middle of a cornfield. I stopped the car, shut the engine off, and enjoyed the beautiful view of the bright full moon in front and above me while sitting in the car (kind of in the middle of cornfield it was). I kept my windows rolled down and enjoyed the warm summer breeze.

"I smoked a cigarette and at some point, I noticed something odd. The sky got a little brighter than it was before, for some reason I started having a very strong urge to leave this place quickly, started looking around (nobody around, only seen maybe one or two cars passed on the highway far behind me) and I noticed it got dead silent in this place.

"Then I noticed it. It was the moon!!! And actually, it couldn't be the moon, because it was located now in a different spot on the dark sky, I also believe it appeared bigger to me than a while ago (couple minutes it takes to smoke a cig). Not really knowing why it scared the hell out of me. Immediately started the car and backed out of that cornfield to highway shoulder and rammed on the gas pedal, I remember looking in the rear-view mirror and seeing the 'Moon' now behind me while it was supposed to be on my right! geeeez ... accelerated like crazy and as fast as I could I started traveling back in Wisconsin Dells downtown direction. For a few minutes I was having this very very scary feeling that the "Moon" was chasing me (maybe it was only trying to scare me off, who knows)... it all lasted maybe 10 minutes. once I left the Route 16 the feeling went away, everything returned to normal. Moon was where it was supposed to be and there was nothing scary anymore. I will remember that feeling for a very long time."

(posted July 21, 2010)

"I was driving on CV road by the Madison, WI airport. As I was driving northbound, I saw a boomerang bright shiny object (a single object) 'appear' immediately in front of my line of sight. I blinked, thinking it might have been something in my eye (I was wearing sunglasses). After blinking the object was no longer there. Then once I finished the 'curve' in CV and headed north...two objects of the same type appeared. As I looked out the window of the car window, they appeared immediately as I looked through the window. The two objects appeared and were visible for about 5 seconds and then just vanished.

"This experience was very weird for me. I am an educated person (two BS degrees and a Masters). It took me a while after the incident to consider reporting this… but something was there for those brief seconds. I saw the first object and then, later, the other two for just those brief seconds. It WAS not an airplane (given that I was driving by the Madison Airport), it was something else."

Wisconsin Reports from NUFORC (National UFO Reporting Center):

Occurred: 6/28/2010 19:00 (Entered as 06/28/10 19:00)
Reported: 6/29/2010 5:39:09 pm 17:39
Posted: 7/6/2010
Location: Platteville, WI
Shape: Cigar
Duration:15mins While driving home we saw a Cigar/ Oval shape, silver object reflecting off the sun in South-western Wisconsin.

On Monday, June 28th, 2010, at approximately 7 pm (1900 hours) we were on our way home from Platteville, Wisconsin southbound on Hwy. 151. I saw something reflecting in the sky that caught my attention and pointed it out to my husband. It was traveling from East to West, was silver, and cigar or oval shape. We kept discussing what we thought it could be since we were intrigued by this "thing" in the sky. There was no contrail from a jet/airplane and it seemed to be hovering at times, so we ruled out that option. My husband then thought it could be the Space Station reflecting off the sun, so we called a friend who then went to the Space Station Tracking site. He called us back and said the Space Station was not in our area at that particular time and the Space Station only travels from West to East. During this time, my husband pulled over the truck so I could look through our binoculars, but I could never find the object when I used them. My husband tried! as well, but our binoculars must not be that magnified. We then continued on our way home, while following this object in the sky. It seemed to move very slowly and would stop and hover. We could still see the object slowly moving when we turned and pulled over on Cty. Rd. O towards home. While traveling on Cty. Rd. O, we lost sight of this silver bright object due to the valley, bluffs, and trees. We never saw it again."

A Triangle /from NUFORC
Occurred: 3/23/2010 20:58 (entered as 03/23/10 20:58)
Reported: 3/23/2010 11:47:57 pm 23:47
Posted: 4/13/2010
Location: Chippewa Falls, WI
Shape: Triangle
Duration: Around 1 Minute Unidentified Triangle shaped craft with lights in each corner, spotted for the 4th time in Chippewa Falls.

March 23, 2010 at 8:58 pm I was on my way to pick up a friend. I was sitting at a stop sign and I am not sure why, but I looked up and I saw a triangle-shaped craft. It had a light on each corner and was moving fast, and it had too low of an altitude to be going as fast as it was. It was low enough to the ground that I can tell you without a doubt that it was not any airplane I have ever seen (My father is in the U.S Military, so I have been to plenty of military bases around the U.S and have seen many planes). It was like I previously stated, a triangle-shaped craft, but made no sound. And at the low altitude the craft was at, and the speed it was flying, I would assume I would have heard some noise. Not far ahead of the craft was an airplane, I believe to be a commuter. The craft made a very sharp, almost 90-degree bank, and headed towards the plane's direction.

This is not the first time I have seen this type of triangle-shaped craft in Chippewa Falls. There have been 3 other encounters with this same type of unidentified craft. This sighting was the first where I have been alone without any witnesses to back up my encounter. The previous 3 had 2 other witnesses not including me in the vehicle at the time.

Another Triangle

Occurred: 6/19/2010 23:10 (entered as 06/19/10 23:10)
Reported: 6/19/2010 9:46:54 pm 21:46
Posted: 6/23/2010
Location: Merrill/Wausau, WI
Shape: Triangle
Duration:1 Min Triangle craft with 3 solid red lights (2 in front, 1 in rear) and 1 solid white light (center), moving low and slowly along the freeway.

We were traveling Northbound on Hwy 51, about 1 mile south of the Hwy 51 Truck Stop, in Merrill, WI. I was driving, looked out of my driver's side window, but towards the front of the vehicle. The craft was about 1 mile away, traveling at a very low speed and a very low altitude, southbound towards our car, parallel to the freeway. The craft had 2 red lights in front of it, and a red light in the rear, center of the two front lights. After the craft passed the car, the 2 front red lights disappeared, and a 4th light, this one white, was in the center of the craft but was only visible from the side and rear of the craft. 3 of us were in the car, and we all saw this craft. There were no sudden movements of the craft, no sound coming from the craft, and none of the lights were flashing, meaning it was not an airplane or helicopter. The craft moved very slowly and smoothly. We followed the highway around a curve, then lost track of it. There were also 3-4 vehicles around us that slowed when we first saw the craft, leaving me to assume they noticed it also.

2011 UFO EVENTS

On January 28, 2011, a UFO is filmed over the Dome of the Rock in Jerusalem.

It was a glowing, pulsating ball of light that descended from the sky and then left by shooting straight up into the air.

On March 28, 2011, lights in a triangular shape are viewed by numerous people in Lafayette, Colorado. The lights are filmed. The triangle headed northeast and faded.

On August 28, 2011, a webcam catches film of a large, rounded, rotating object in the air over a marina on Long Island, New York.

Budd Hopkins, longtime UFOlogist and author of *Witnessed*, dies on August 21, 2011. (June 15, 1931–August 21, 2011).

Local Sightings

Date of Incident: July 13th, 2008
Time of Incident: 11:00 am

Location of Incident: Westby, Vernon County
Source of Report: UFOWisconsin.com online sightings report by Brad A.
Details of Incident

I just happened to be looking at the clouds, when I saw a silver cigar-shaped object come out of a cloud. At first, I just thought it was part of the cloud until I noticed it was moving much faster than the clouds were. Then when I got up to get a better look at it, the object changed direction and started moving south until it eventually disappeared. The object made no sound and it didn't appear to have any wings. (http://www.ufowisconsin.com)

National UFO Reporting Center
Sighting Report Occurred: 12/10/2010 10:08 (Entered as 12/10/2010 10:08)
Reported: 12/13/2010 8:10:11 pm 20:10
Posted: 1/5/2011
Location: Boscobel, WI
Shape: Circle
Duration: hours Over Boscobel, Wisconsin 3 blue and red flashing objects staying in one place in the sky
Date of Incident: 6/2005
Time of Incident: Dusk
Location of Incident: Hillsboro, Vernon County
Other Related Reports: Not Applicable
Source of Report: UFOWisconsin.com online sightings report form by Paul M
Details of Incident

I was walking on a small country road about five miles outside Hillsboro, WI, at about dusk. Upon reaching the top of a hill, I spotted perhaps five or six bright lights very high up in the distant northern sky. I immediately knew they weren't stars, because they had the intensity of bright electric sources, and were ranged in a perfect line. The sun had sunk past the horizon, but the clear sky hadn't dimmed enough for the stars to come out fully.

The lights vanished after glowing, apparently motionless, for a few seconds. I stood where I was and continued watching. Sure enough, the lights returned—only a little to the east. They glowed for a few moments, then disappeared again. A minute passed, and I saw one of the lights turn on again, a bit more to the west. In response, the rest lit up beside it, in a perfectly straight row. They blinked out simultaneously. The lights kept replaying the blink-and-answer routine for the next few minutes, at irregular intervals, their positions changing. First, I'd see them a little east of where I'd seen them before, and then they'd pop up west of there. Sometimes it looked as if they were coming closer, and at other times I thought they were moving away. I heard no sound, nor did I actually witness any movement. They just kept reappearing in different places.

The last time I saw them, the lights turned on in a row running almost exactly north and south, much farther away, disappearing into the north. With my cell phone, I called my brother, who lives with me, and told him about the lights. He's a great skeptic about such things, but to his credit, he believed me. He ran out to see them for himself, but the lights had gone by the time he joined me.

Sighting Report Occurred: 6/20/2005 21:00 (Entered as 06/20/2005 21:00)

Reported: 6/20/2005 8:37:29 pm 20:37
Posted: 6/20/2005
Location: Galesville, WI
Shape: Formation
Duration: 20 min

The objects were dark and circular. They would disappear and then reappear in a different location. One object seemed to be in the shape of a dome on top. I saw one, then two and three. There were most usually two. The odd thing is that as I was taking pictures of these dark objects, I began to notice the clouds changing a ways toward the right of them. I took three pictures of the changing formation. I was using a digital camera and when I took the picture of the large configuration, my camera went totally black except for the normal information readout. I have never had this happen before. I tried repeatedly to take a picture and it just wouldn't work. Even the viewfinder was black. I had to turn it off and then turn it on again. By that time the large configuration was gone.

Occurred: 6/7/2005 21:30 (Entered as 06/07/2005 21:30)
Reported: 6/11/2005 8:49:20 pm 20:49
Posted: 6/20/2005
Location: Mauston, WI
Shape: Light
Duration: 4 seconds. Four large horizontal red lights in Mauston, WI. Starts as 4 lights, goes to 2 lights, and then disappears.

At Woodside Ranch attending a conference. Myself and two others were in the pool when one of my friends said to look in the sky. Myself and my other friend turned to the northern sky to see four red lights in a horizontal line. They were above the tree line and were very large. They were not like lights on an airplane, they were much, much larger. There were four lights and then it went to just two lights (the end lights went out). After it went to two lights, they went out and it disappeared. We never really made out a space craft, we only saw the lights in the horizontal formation. My friends and I believe we saw a UFO, but the fact that we saw what we believe to be 2 military jets fly by about ten minutes after the sighting made us wonder if the object was related to the jets and a military mission. But it also made us wonder if the jets were sent to investigate the object that was seen. Who knows, but we know we saw something very, very unusual. I've never ever even thought I've seen a UFO in my entire life, but when I saw this object, I had no doubt that I had just seen something that could be one. I would love to be contacted by an investigator to see if anyone else saw this thing or for information on what it could have been.

National UFO Reporting Center
Sighting Report Occurred: 8/14/2011 23:18 (Entered as 08/14/11 23:18)
Reported: 8/19/2011 12:04:44 pm 12:04
Posted: 8/21/2011
Location: Baraboo, WI
Shape: Fireball
Duration: 3 min. 4 to 5 Firey flying objects, stopping then fading away. 8-14-2011 11:18 pm Baraboo, Wisconsin

My wife and I were camping in Wisconsin Dells, Jelly Stone Park Campground. On August 14, 2011, at approximately 11:18 pm, my wife and I were walking our dog, Chance, down Ishnala Rd. As we walked, something in the sky caught our eye, it was an orangish/reddish/fiery object coming over the tree line to our left which was a slightly northwest direction.

This object came over the tree line at a plane-like speed heading slightly southeast. It slowed down to a complete stop in the sky and started to flicker and fade away. As that one was fading, a second one started to come over the tree line following the same flight pattern and movements precisely, stopping at the same point the first one we spotted (by that time the first one was gone) and started the same phase, flickering then fading. This continued at least two to three more times for a total of at least four or five times, then stopped.

As we were watching, there was a third person driving down Ishnala Road at a slow speed. As he approached, he stopped and was in awe as my wife and I were at seeing this. We both tried to figure out what these objects could possibly be and cannot come up with an earthly reasonable response. Therefore, I do believe in extraterrestrial life forms from this point on.

National UFO Reporting Center
Sighting Report Occurred: 8/11/2011 17:58 (Entered as 08/11 /11 17:58)
Reported: 8/11/2011 4:21:37 pm 16:21
Posted: 8/21/2011
Location: West Salem, WI
Shape: Circle
Duration: 5 sec round sphere moving fast through the sky.

We were sitting on the back porch as a dark small rain cloud rolled in providing a nice contest to the sky. Looking up I saw a softball-shaped craft move toward the northwest at an unusually fast speed. No sound report came from it. When it cleared the clouds, its shape was clearly identifiable as a round ball shape. It moved out of view after five seconds.

No airport traffic was reported in the area.

2012 UFO EVENTS

A secret UFO research program that was initiated by Senator Harry Reid ended in 2012. It had operated on a budget of 22 million dollars in annual funding. Called the Advanced Aviation Threat Identification Program, it is believed by some observers that the program continues in another form.

Local Sightings:
Three stories from one man, formerly from Readstown

Story #1

OK, John, this happened to me in 1984 while I was coon hunting. I was hunting about 3 miles east of Westby. I talked to the farmer and he told me, I was the only person that was supposed to be on his land. So, if I seen anybody else out there, I was to tell them to get off his land. So, I parked on the edge of a long field and walked the field out to the woods, As I was halfway across the field I notice a light about 8 to 12 feet off the ground, moving through the trees real slow. I thought it was a truck with its roof lights on. It was going real slow and the light was a reddish-orange. I had 2 Dura-Beam lanterns that I used for spotting coon. So, I thought I would go over and find out who was hunting on this guy's land. I was about 100 yards away when I turned my light on him. The light stopped and slowly rose to the top of the trees. And then it followed the tree tops down into the valley and disappeared. It made no noise. I ran over to the edge of the woods, but it was gone.

Story # 2

In about 1975 I went coon hunting about 1 mile west of Readstown. It was about 3 am and I noticed a light in the sky. I thought it was a slow-moving airplane. As I walked across the ridge top I noticed this light was staying behind me. But it was long way off. As I got to the edge of the field, the light went over my head and stopped on the edge of the woods on the other side of the valley and stayed there for over half an hour. As I was walking in my driveway, this fog appeared, it so thick I couldn't see more than 3 feet in front of me. Then all of a sudden the fog was gone and so was the light.

Story #3

I was working in La Crosse on the night shift. The day after 9-11 all planes were not supposed to fly except for police and emergency aircraft. About 12:50 am. I noticed this light and it was moving real slow. It made no noise. It went right over my head, I figured it was about 1000 ft so up in the sky. It took a right turn so sharp, that no plane made could do. It went about a quarter mile and made another turn the right and flew off the way it came from. In my duties at work, I had to make hourly trips outside. I went out about 1:20 am. or so and I noticed this light again. I thought to myself, what is this thing? So, I made a mark in the parking lot and measured this light to see if it turned in the same place every time, I measured the light using the other buildings around me. I watched this thing leave and come back. It took 13 minutes to do its round trip. It turned in the same place every time. I ran inside and told one of my co-workers to come watch this thing. I had a pair of binoculars 20 x 60 power. The light was flashing a white light, but with the binoculars you could see 3 white lights, one on each tip of the craft, with a long pole hanging under it. With the naked eye, all you could see was the flashing light. I asked my friend who was in the service at one time, what the heck this was. All he could say was "it's no airplane" he didn't have a clue what it was. I even hit it with a spotlight and couldn't see the craft. I watched it come and go until about 4:30 in the morning. The sun was coming up and the morning fog was rolling in, but I did see it on the last round. It was triangle-shaped, until it got over my head, and then it looked like a horseshoe shape. When you see these things, nobody believes you. Even people that have seen things will contradict what you say.

From MUFON website from Boscobel, Wis.

I had just arrived home from working my second shift job. I arrived home at 1130 pm, grabbed a bite to eat, and went outside around 1 am to have a cigarette. It was a beautiful star-filled night and we have a huge backyard

so as I normally do I look up at the stars just for fun. it was a full moon, though I believe it was relatively low in the sky that night as I remember. I was looking up at the stars something caught my eye to my northeast. I thought it was a plane coming at first. it was a huge black object, almost boomerang-shaped and it was so huge that I could trace it in the dark because it was covering up the stars in the sky as it moved. it was moving very slowly and made no noise as it passed by and had no navigation lights on it either. it almost looked like a stealth bomber but it was so low and had no exhaust emission that I believe it was not an air-force aircraft. I watched it move slowly until it was out of my viewing range. it sent chills down my spine and I had a really strange feeling about it as soon as it happened. I feel that this was no normal aircraft for many reasons. no blinking lights, no noise, and it was very low in the sky. It was just so huge and the reason I can tell that is because the way it covered up so many of the stars in the sky and it being so bright out, I could make out every characteristic of the craft. I just want my story out there and maybe someone else has seen a similar object. My best friend is a Staff Sergeant in the US Air Force so I am familiar with most planes, even drones like my friend works on. This was no plane and being so far from a major airport and air base makes that out of the question in my mind. I would like any information your group may provide and wouldn't mind joining the MUFON network as I am now a firm believer in the existence of objects out of this world. Thank you
May 2012

Also on the MUFON website from Boscobel

Last night about 10:15 I was letting the dogs in from outside when I noticed two bright amber lights going south to north. I was watching them and they didn't blink and were moving quite fast. All of a sudden one faded out as if shutting a light off. I came in and went out on the deck in front and there came another one. I yelled for the wife to come see the UFO and she came out and saw it too. Soon yet another one came and they all seemed to follow the same flight pattern and they made no noise whatsoever. I went in and grabbed the camera and went out to the backyard and waited. Nothing came for quite a while. She went back in because the mosquitoes were bad so I went to the front deck. Having my camera set on video mode and waiting. Then two more came and I headed to the backyard away from the big tree in front. When I got to the back the second light was gone, but I captured the one on video. It was a very bright amber light, not blinking. When I played back the video it shows the light, but it's flashing green and blue as well.

The UFO was flying in a straight path but the video shows it jumping around. That is me trying to keep it in the viewfinder.

June 2012

A Man from the Central Kickapoo Valley

It was February 2012 about 4:30 in the afternoon. I was returning home after working in Platteville. North of Boscobel on highway 61, as I was coming out of the valley and reaching the top of the hill near Mt Zion that's when I spotted it. It was still light enough out that you couldn't see any stars in the sky as the sun was not yet set. Three bright lights yellow in color in a triangle formation (one in front flanked by the other two) appeared to the right at 45 degrees and traveled from the east to west at a high rate of speed and disappeared. They made no sound that I could hear and traveled faster than anything that I have ever seen in the sky.

From MUFON website, from Hillsboro, Wis.

In a remote rural area in Vernon County, Wisconsin, on a dark clear night, observed a red steady light followed by a white globe light alternating from bright to dim at regular intervals. First observed the lights at about 40 degrees over the north horizon, traveling in a straight line due south until it disappeared to the south horizon. Emitting from the object were yellow/orange fireballs similar to military weapon tracer rounds toward the east and west at erratic sequence intervals. This object continued on a steady course. Total time of travel was about 20-30 seconds. Because there were no reference points it is unknown what speed or altitude this object was traveling. There was no sound. I am a USAF veteran, come from a family of WW-2 pilots, airline pilots, and flight instructors. I have much aviation experience myself and still fly ultra-lights. Never saw anything like this object before.

Sept. 2012

A woman from the central Kickapoo Valley, now of Madison

The night was cloudless. The sky was endlessly black, with stars so bright that you think you can reach out and touch them. It was a crisp fall evening along Highway 14, at the top of Sugar Grove Hill.

I was in the car with a friend, taking a little spin for no particular reason, other than we were new to the freedom of having drivers' licenses. As we drove toward Readstown, we noticed a series of white lights in the sky. We looked at one another, asking almost simultaneously "Do you see that?". We both nodded that we did and then pulled over along the side of the road. The lights moved slowly along the horizon in a straight line. We didn't speak, not knowing what we were seeing or what we should say. After less than one minute, the white lights disappeared as quickly as they appeared, leaving us to wonder if it had all been in our imaginations.

No, it wasn't. I remember it to this day and have had one or two similar experiences since that night so many years ago. Still, as I think fondly of my growing up years in the Kickapoo Valley, I reflect back on the marvel of it, in a most marvelous area.

From National UFO Reporting Center website
Occurred: 9/9/2012 04:30 (Entered as 09/09/2012 04:30)
Reported: 9/9/2012 3:14:24 pm 15:14
Posted: 9/24/2012
Location: La Crosse, WI
Shape: Diamond
Duration: 5 minutes

Saw two triangle shapes flying and doing odd things then got close and disappeared.

From Petersfield, England Post about the picture of crop circle

The pattern is about 250 metres in size and appears to be a labyrinth design, which historically has been used for religious, ritual, and magic purposes.

Lucy Pringle, a founder member of the Centre for Crop Circle Studies in Sheet, said the mile-long endless looping pattern is the "best this year."

She said, "To me, its labyrinth design represents our journey through life. I think it's beyond the wit of man to produce something as intricate as this, as its geometric precision is highly accurate. But however it got there, to me it personifies the wonderful spirit of the Olympic Games."

2013 UFO EVENTS

At the Citizens Hearing on Disclosure, Paul Hellyer, the former Canadian Minister of Defense testified that aliens are real and it is likely that two of them are working within the U.S. government. He asserts that at least four species of aliens have been visiting Earth for thousands of years.

Local Sightings
The Readstown Lights—one night in September

A Man from Readstown
It was about 9:30 pm on sept. 11, 2013 I was standing in my front yard and I saw a formation of white lights come down from the direction of Viroqua. I counted 13 lights. they were all white, not colored. They came from Viroqua and headed east. Over the western side of Readstown, they did a loop and turned south. They kept going south until I could not see them anymore. they made no noise.

Was this part of a display of ornamental floating balloons set off the same night as a memorial?

John S (from Facebook): "Some were of the opinion that it was Japanese lanterns which had apparently been launched by someone in the area."

Local woman: "We sent lanterns off in Readstown on Sept 11, 2013 in our roof, my Granddaughter that passed away a year ago on that date, we set off 47 of them."

John S.: "What time did you launch them? And from where?"

Local woman: "7:45 til about 9 pm, Readstown Cemetery."

Elsewhere on the same night (on National UFO Reporting Center)
Occurred: 9/11/2013 23:30 (Entered as 09/11/13 23:30)
Reported: 9/12/2013 2:21:16 pm 14:21
Posted: 9/30/2013
Location: Scottsdale, AZ
Shape: Other
Duration: hour and a half+

I saw a cluster of white lights from 11:30 pm-1:00 am slowly moving across the sky.

At around 11:30 pm on September 11, 2013, I saw an unfamiliar cluster of white lights in the sky. They looked like stars, so I just assumed I hadn't noticed them before. But around midnight I noticed that the cluster seemed to have moved slightly from where it was earlier. I paid close attention to it from midnight until almost 1:00 am, and it was moving very slowly across the sky. From 11:30 pm-1:00 am, it moved about 5-6 inches in the sky.

I spent about an hour on the internet trying to find what this could be - satellites, weather balloons,—but I couldn't find anything. However, I noticed that the lights were in a similar formation to the Pleiades star cluster. But I did research on that and I didn't find anything that mentioned the Pleiades star cluster moving.

I left around 1:00 am, so it could have been there much longer. I'm going to go out tonight and see if it's there again.

Mysterious Triangles, here and elsewhere on the same night

A Man from the Soldiers Grove area

The first real incident was on April 6, 2011. It was right at dusk about 8 pm. I was at my house to the south of Soldiers Grove. I was outside looking for UFOs because I had had conversations with friends in Viroqua about them that day to the effect that they had seen things in the sky and wanted to see what I could see myself.

For several minutes I stood outside in the darkness with no success. I finally put out the message with my gut, not my voice, that "if you are out here, I want to see you." And then a white dot appeared and began to move. At first, I thought it was a falling star, but gradually it moved toward me. Very rapidly it became a triangle of lights—one bright light on each corner of a triangle. It was half materialized—you could see stars through it. There was a swirling mass of gas in the center—perhaps this was something connected to the propulsion. The triangle was about 100 feet long on each side. The thickness was 15 to 20 feet. I watched it for about fifteen minutes when it left. I felt complete friendliness from them—the craft said goodbye to me and left.

Since then, I have seen about thirty other craft. I invited them in and they have been visiting. Once I saw two little beings in my living room after a sighting of their craft outside, but otherwise, I have not seen any entities. Nothing very strange or bad has come about as a result of all this. Since then I have been reading books on the subject such as *Return of the Bird Tribes* by Ken Carey *and The Gaia Project* by Hwee-Yong Jang.

From NUFORC website, both dated April 6, 2011

Occurred: 4/6/2011 17:00 (Entered as 04/06/11 17:00)
Reported: 4/6/2011 10:05:01 pm 22:05
Posted: 5/2/2011
Location: Las Vegas, NV
Shape: Triangle
Duration:10 Minutes
Triangle-shaped UFO hovers overhead.

We were out in the desert where we usually go to look for UFOs when this triangle-shaped object appeared overhead, it didn't make a sound, and it hovered for about 10 minutes before disappearing, definitely not a plane, and we were the only people around.

When it left a few fighter jets flew around the area, as if they were looking for something.

Occurred: 4/6/2011 01:00 (Entered as 04/06/2011 1:00)
Reported: 5/5/2011 9:38:47 pm 21:38
Posted: 5/12/2011
Location: Mystic, CT
Shape: Triangle
Duration: 5-6 mins

I saw a triangle UFO in the Mystic, CT hotel area.

When I was standing outside my job at a hotel in Mystic, Connecticut, a coworker and I were outside smoking cigarettes, and we looked up into the sky where we saw a hovering light, as we watched the light, it started to move upward, straight up, we did nothing but watch as this light raised up high, then it started moving towards us, as it was moving the light patterns changed, several times they changed, then once it was right above us, the lights changed into a six dot pyramid, during this whole event, there was no sound at all, after that, it just flew away.

Lights on the Coon Valley Hill
A Man from Readstown

About 1999 I was on my way to La Crosse, it was about 10 pm. Just west of Coon Valley I noticed this object which I thought was a low flying plane. All of a sudden it stopped and reversed direction. I hurried to the top of the hill to see what it was. It crossed the road in front of me and flew across the field about 50 feet off the ground. It had red blinking lights all over it. I estimated it was about 50 feet across and 30 feet high. And it didn't make a sound.

An Orange Sphere in the 1970s
A Man from Readstown

This was probably about 1972 or 73. I was driving from Viroqua to Viola at about 10 pm. After I passed Liberty, I saw an object over the hill to the north of the road. I saw it as I began to climb the hill. This object was hovering over the hill, and then suddenly it was gone. It wasn't a bouncing light in the light that people talk about. It was orange in color was definitely a saucer. It had no lights but was illuminated from within. It was about a half to 3/4 of a mile away from me. When it left I did not see it travel, it was just was there and then it wasn't there. It could have headed north or it could have just disappeared. I don't know.

2014 UFO EVENTS

U.S. Navy pilots reported seeing strange objects with no discernible engine reaching 30,000 feet altitude and traveling at hypersonic speed. The objects were making sudden stops and instantaneous turns — something beyond the physical limits of a human crew. This was off the East Coast of the U.S.

Local Sightings

A Woman from Viroqua

You may think I am certifiable after I relate what I just observed.

I stood outside at approx. 11:30 pm and watched a small light in the southern sky above the trees shoot down and up and zig-zag and right and left through the sky. It appears to have red and blue/green lights that blink sporadically. Sometimes there is a flash and flare trail as it moves. It is erratic and goes sometimes in a triangle shape, sometimes back and forth or up and down. No particular pattern to its movements.

I watched it for 10 minutes and then came in, understandably spooked. I went back out 15 minutes later and it had moved somewhat towards the west but still mostly in the southern sky. It is not moving like a satellite or airplane.

Came in and wrote this and...checked again...okay... now it's gone. All the usual stars are there but nothing is moving about as this thing did. No, I had no wine or anything else tonight. And I hesitate to post this because it sounds pretty crazy. But I did see IT!

"They" are out there. Yes, I know that some of you are now convinced I am a bit loopy. It's okay. I know what I saw.

A Woman from Star Valley

My neighbor has stories of UFO sightings in Star Valley. I often peruse the night sky looking for dark cigar-shaped clouds hovering. I scrutinize satellites and anything blinking hoping to be allowed into this club. While I was living in Ireland years ago, we once chased flashing lights down a dark lane into an empty field. I fell asleep in a bluebell field and was woken up by a kiss from a little man who shimmered a glowing white. But that is like a fairytale dream. I wanted proof.

Last May I became a full believer. It didn't happen at night. I wasn't even looking. The sky was blue, a warm blue that goes on forever without a cloud to interrupt it. I was straightening up the woodpile. I stood up with an armload of wood and noticed the moon hovering in the sky. I looked closer. It looked like the moon, but with its ends cut off, making it more of a triangle than a crescent. It was white, the same tone that the moon has in the daytime sky. Then I realized I was looking north. The moon is never in the north sky. The shape didn't move. I was very puzzled and didn't take my eyes off of it. A plane came out of the west on a path that would intersect with this white shape. As the plane got close to the object, this white shape suddenly moved in a fast tight loop. It disappeared behind the trunk of a tree and I watched closely to catch it when it reappeared on the other side of it. It didn't reappear. It disappeared.

I knew for certain I had seen something that couldn't be explained. I thought it looked like it flew away from the airplane. Then I thought how weird it was that the airplane was there. It was not an ordinary plane. It was low and flying at a strange angle. I know the planes over this valley. They come and they go, flying high over the valley. This plane was low and green. I wish I had taken a moment to look at the plane more, but I was so focused on that white shape hovering in the sky. I like to believe that the other plane saw it too, that it was a military plane assigned to chase it out of here. I'd like to believe that what I saw was documented, even if they don't want to release that type of information to the public. I'd like to believe that I am now a member of this club.

From NUFORC (National UFO Reporting Center) database

Occurred: 8/2/2014 21:00 (Entered as 08/02/14 21:00)
Reported: 8/5/2014 5:39:57 pm 17:39
Posted: 8/8/2014
Location: De Soto, WI
Shape: Fireball

Duration: 3 minutes

Two big, bright, silent, non-blinking orange fireball-type lights cross Mississippi River valley near De Soto, WI.

Approximately 9:00 pm on Saturday, August 2, 2014, two large, bright, non-blinking, silent orange fireball-type lights flew over the Mississippi River valley from the Iowa side to near the town of De Soto, Wisconsin.

The first light flew quickly and as it came to the Wisconsin side of the river turned northeast and rapidly faded from view.

The second light came right on its heels. This light moved much slower and followed the exact same flight path as the first.

We brainstormed the possibilities of what the lights could have been and both agreed that we had never seen anything like them before.

Occurred: 6/13/2014 23:10 (Entered as : 06/13/2014 23:10)

Reported: 6/14/2014 3:48:27 pm 15:48

Posted: 6/20/2014

Location: Onalaska, WI

Shape: Triangle

Duration: 3 minutes

I went outside to get a view of the full Honey Moon.

Saw triangle craft hovering and then slowly moved north. orangish, red and blue lights pulsing...no noise.

I ran into my house to get a camera, but it disappeared by the time I got outside.

It was not an airplane, however the week before several military helicopters were flying over about the same time of night. You could hear and see that they were helicopters. I have no idea what this was.

Occurred: 11/13/2013 19:30 (Entered as 11/13/13 19:30)
Reported: 11/13/2013 7:23:01 pm 19:23
Posted: 11/20/2013 NUFORC
Location: La Crosse, WI
Shape: Triangle
Duration: 10 seconds

We were driving northwest on HWY 14/61 towards La Crosse and saw a solid-looking, dark gray, silent triangle pass over us. The triangle appeared slim and solid, it also appeared to have a dim bluish light at each point of the flying triangle. It was flying just a few feet above the treetops near the highway. It also seemed to be silent as is passed above us.

Occurred: 11/3/2013 20:00 (Entered as 11/03/13 20:00)
Reported: 11/3/2013 7:16:26 pm 19:16
Posted: 11/11/2013 NUFORC
Location: Tomah, WI
Shape: Triangle
Duration: 10-20 seconds

Triangular shape craft with 5 lights, 1 at each point and 1 in-between each side on the front of the craft. It almost seemed slightly transparent but could still see the craft. I just happened to be looking at the sky at the right time you could hardly see it the lights were really dim white lights that were not flashing and the craft made no sound. The craft was big. I wonder if it is military with the transparency but still able to see it.

2015 UFO EVENTS

Chinese city in the sky debunked.

Signs of water found on Mars.

Observation of Kepler satellite sparks speculation of ET structures in space.

Scientist Stephan Hawking expressed pessimistic viewpoints regarding ET intervention in planet Earth activities: "If aliens visit us, the outcome could be much like when Columbus landed in America, which didn't turn out well for the Native Americans," Professor Hawking was quoted as saying.

The Vatican Chief Astronomer has confirmed that the Vatican Observatory believes in the existence of life on other planets.

In May mysterious UFOs were filmed over San Diego, Siberia, and at a PGA golf tournament in Florida.

Clusters of red and orange lights were reported in various places throughout the year.

Local Sightings
(From MUFON website)

Long Description of Sighting Report

I was with two friends driving north from Walmart in Prairie du Chien Wisconsin And noticed lights over a smoke tower that previously had no lights on it and when we approached the tower we pulled into a Dairy Q And when telling the story tomorrow to friends there are more than 5 people that have seen the same object multiple times in the same time between a parking lot and got out of the vehicle and noticed a triangle-shaped object making no noise floating above the MLPs smoke tower of the Prairie du Chien prison We watch the object hover for more than 5 to 10 minutes and suddenly it took off faster than anything I've ever seen in my life and disappeared over the horizon within 1 to 2 seconds After speaking with multiple people there are more than five to ten people that I've seen the same object multiple times in the same area over the prison. And I have seen it on one other occasion about a mile from my residence.
2006-05-15
8:00 pm seen

NUFORC Website

Occurred: 11/30/2014 15:58 (Entered as 11/30/14 15:58)
Reported: 12/30/2014 8:51:30 pm 20:51
Posted: 1/7/2015
Location: Lynxville, WI
Shape: Circle
Duration: 2.5 minutes

It was 15:58 pm The last day of deer season. I'm sitting in my truck, watching 2 fields for deer. Facing due east. From possibly 15 degrees north/northeast and possibly 10 miles away, a round disk-shaped object came from N/E Iowa at probably Mach 2. It had a white hue around its front. The sun was at my back. The object was like polished stainless steel. It came to a dead stop one-half mile due east of me and hung in the air for about 2 minutes. After it stopped the hue went away. It looked like the cover of a Revere Ware saucepan, on its edge. After about 2 minutes, the thing turned 90 degrees and gave a huge, bright, white flash and then disappeared. Its elevation was less than 1000 feet. There were cirrus clouds in an otherwise clear afternoon. Comparing its size to a farmhouse behind it, I estimate it to be about 30 feet in diameter—It was approximately 1/2 mile from my position. I had a cell phone and a camera on my center console, but never even thought about taking a pic.
((NUFORC Note: Witness elects to remain totally anonymous; provides no contact information. PD))

Occurred: 12/31/2014 17:25 (Entered as 12/31/2014 17:25)
Reported: 1/24/2015 9:38:42 am 09:38
Posted: 1/26/2015
Location: Readstown, WI
Shape: Chevron
Duration: 2 minutes

Bright quarter Moon-shaped object over a ridge top, entirely lit up over and over, almost like a series of photos in the sky.

We had a dinner reservation at 5:30 pm on New Year's Eve, so at 5:25 pm I went outside to get the car started and warm. It was dark. On the way to the car, I saw an object looking like a quarter moon with the bottom left corner filled in.

The object moved over a hillside, just over the top of the hill. It finally went behind the trees but I could still see the light from it. It was almost as large as the trees.

The object moved in a jerky fashion, almost like I was looking at a series of photographs projected in the sky, in first a westward direction, and later north, behind the trees on top of the hill.

I watched it for about 30 seconds from the driveway, and then when it disappeared behind the trees I walked out in the yard where I could still see the light it made for a few more seconds. It was not the moon, which was in the western sky.

On the same night, New Year's Eve 2014/15 came this similar sighting in Australia:

UFO Sighting Reported Over East Maitland, NSW, Australia On New Year's Eve 2015

According to eyewitness testimony, "I saw one bright light orange/amber light, slowly moving in a set direction. I lost track of it in the trees and a few seconds later as I got past the trees it had completely disappeared." (from UFOblogger.com)

Occurred: 11/6/2014 21:00 (Entered as 11.6/2014 21:00)
Reported: 11/7/2014 3:43:44 pm 15:43
Posted: 11/14/2014
Location: Onalaska, WI
Shape: Circle

UFO sighting in Onalaska, WI.

I was driving to school to pick up my daughter from a concert. I could see light far away behind the trees. First saw it was a plane, but the lights did not seem to move. I thought it was strange that a plane would move that slow.

As I kept driving, I got a clear view, and realized it was a round object at about 7,000 ft. (not sure) It had square color lights around it. The lights took turns flashing brighter than the others, but it was not at a fast speed. Or maybe the object was moving in circles but it was very slow, as it seemed to be sitting still in the air. I kept driving to my destination so not sure how long it remained in place. Also, since there was not too much activity around me, I feared a little, and just wanted to find a place to be safe.

From N.

2016 UFO EVENTS

Democratic Presidential candidate Hillary Clinton hints that she might release UFO information if she is elected president. Republican Donald Trump makes no such promises. Clinton's campaign manager is John Podesta. He is a long-time UFO exposure advocate.

On April 8, 2016, traffic on a highway in Guangzhou, China came to a standstill as a saucer passed over the road. Numerous people filmed it with cellphones and dashboard cameras.

On May 13, 2016, a light was filmed over Fairbanks, Alaska which shot out multiple balls of light.

Local Sightings

POYNT GUARD (from a Man from Viroqua)

For some writers, the stories take years to evolve, starting first as just an idea, a vision, a snapshot, a sketch, a picture, which may take time to speed up into motion...

I first introduced myself to the readers of this paper in my writing of "From Whence it Came" published in

Epitaph-News of Viola, Wisconsin, U.S.A., UFOs of the Kickapoo #15, special to the newspaper by John H.Sime, dated, Oct. 28, 2004.

In that story, I wrote of how I used to work as a caretaker of several properties in northern Richland County, Wisconsin.

This story is of one area which is in the Township of Henrietta.

The meaning of the word Henrietta is "Gift of the MAG (J) I" as I have come to understand it.

Anyway...here is the story from that township.

My two friends, whose names I shall not mention, purchased a property there in 1976.

In the fall of 1978, we began the construction of a small geodesic dome home on the east-facing hillside, within twenty feet of a spring that flowed from an aquifer located within Fox Ridge. Soon the place was completed into a comfortable living space.

A few years later, while there, I would sometimes keep trout in a small bucket, beneath the pipe from where the water flowed out of the spring. I had caught the trout from the stream across the highway.

One morning, I noticed that a beautiful 12.5 inch brook trout had vanished from the small pool. I searched the immediate area and could not find it. What had become of it, I thought? I soon realized, a-ha, an owl had come and snatched it as its yellowish-orange and white dark aqua-blue-green self-moved slowly, near the surface of the pail in the light of the almost full moon.

From then on, I always kept an old wire net fish basket on the top of the pail if trout were residing within, which was, of course, a very rare occurrence.

Through the years, many friends and acquaintances came and went from that place, spending our time there lovingly. None was better for me than my brief time there with Jezabble, a wondrous woman, who first came seeking a "vision quest".

None of us stayed there very long except for my two friends who had originally purchased the property. For quite a few years they were at another place in the U.S.A., working.

Eventually, they returned.

One night, the male of the two exclaimed to me as we sat around the campfire: "Well, while you were living here, did you ever see THEM?"

"Them what?" I said.

He began to tell me that when he and his wife first purchased the property, they, his sister, and some friends were sitting on top of the hill above, on the rock out-cropping.

They observed four separate, floating, pale-white, oblong, somewhat egg-shaped, luminous objects moving slowly about the waterways and springs that adorn the valley floor across the highway.

Some of that land, over 200 acres, was then and is now, owned by the State of Wisconsin, the D.N.R.

My experience with THEM, I've related to few others until now!

During the Winter of 1986, I was alone in the dome one night. While in a deep sleep I may have been dreaming, but ever so slowly, I began to waken. I could not move—dream paralysis, happened.

I was able to open my eyes and SEE four objects, as described above, slightly below the ceiling of the room.

They began moving toward me. I lay motionless. I wanted to scream, call out, move, but I could not. I felt frightened. All four inched closer, closer, closer, until they were right in front of my face!

Suddenly, I was fully awake, totally calm, and able to move myself and my limbs. I lay there for a while, how long I can't recall.

That is where my recognition of events goes blank. It was as if my TV set picture turned to gray and white shimmering snow, swirled by a whirling windmillistic movement of emptiness, yet also of oneness. I had a feeling of emptiness because my friends were not there to support me. But I felt a oneness with the Earth and sky.

It is a oneness that permeates my being to this day.

I had people in my life at that time, with whom I was acquainted, but lacked significant others nearby.

I have many fond memories overall of that part of the Earth, sky, and the time I spent there with the many beings, creatures, birds, fish, deer, and humans, etc. that I encountered.

Soon thereafter, my life changed. My Pinto wagon stopped running and had to be towed to the local "boneyard" for no longer useful vehicles.

I decided to return again to the "old fashioned" means of transport—walking. I formed new friendships with the many people I met along "the path", the highway.

Despite all of this, I remained happy. The trout were biting well. The winter was waning down, the days were getting longer, warmer and I had my harmonicas and my splendid musical vocalizations to entertain both myself and the creatures of the forest. I could sing and play as loud as I wanted for there were no human neighbors living close enough to complain of the "noise".

So, you might ask, what did the human neighbors say amongst themselves about this "vagabond" in their midst? Those stories, depending on who is telling them, vary and remain in a haze, such as one might find in the fog of a cool coming of dawn, along a long forgotten waterway.

Soon, my life began to vastly improve. I began to thrive, meet new people, expand on my musical talents and my skills as a human services provider.

I continued to follow my bliss and doors opened to foster me further toward my dreams and wonderment.

And with that, I shall conclude.

It has been written by many that in the BEGINNING—DEUS EX MACHINA—of ancient Greek dramaturgy:

Perhaps, at a Garden of Eden so to speak; we all came forth from Four entities of LUMINOUS LIGHTNESS.

There *had* to be TWO SEPARATE "COUPLES". One Adam, one Eve, and another Adam, and Eve, or else not to sound crude or anything we would all be too closely related.

Ponder these thoughts for a while if you choose...

So there, no you have it. This story is merely a glimpse, or suggestion, possibly a window for viewing.

Take this story and run with it where you will, if you want to, in the land of milk and honey.

Respectfully submitted. June 30, 2016, AM—DAWN.

A Man from Readstown

Last week (first week of October 2016) I saw an amber or orange-colored shape over the south end of Nelson's Hill in Readstown (west of the Kickapoo River), sort of over the new bridge. It was just about dusk.

The object was not round, it was rectangular. It must have been at least thirty feet long. It was not an airplane shape.

It stayed still in the sky for about a minute. Then it gradually moved right (north) down in front of the hill. Finally, it went back up and moved to the west. It disappeared after another minute.

A Man from Readstown

It was still summer in 2008 or 2007. It was daylight, about 2:30 pm. It was right straight above the Boaz Country Store, in the middle of the sky. We were heading west toward Readstown going down the Bashford Hill.

My passenger saw it first. It was a real object, not a light. It was very shiny, the rays of the sun were bouncing off it, making a rainbow effect. It is hard to say how big was it. It is hard to compare it to anything. It was stationary. I was driving so I didn't get to study it closely. I did not see it take off. I pulled the car off into the gravel, we both got out and it was gone. We both were certain it was nothing earthly.

From MUFON (Mutual UFO Network)

On September 9, 2016, following report was submitted from Ferryville, Wis. (object seen that day):

"Traveling south during a rainstorm when rain diminished, I saw two red globes above river bluffs. a few miles further south I saw a red globe over water. one had a white globe on either side of the red globe and was low over the water."

2017 UFO EVENTS

In fall, 2017, an object first spotted by an observatory in Hawaii, which was given the Hawaiian name *Oumuamua* (scout), passed through our solar system. Numerous astronomers speculated that it could be some kind of ET craft on an exploratory mission.

Local Sightings

A Witness from Soldiers Grove

This was about three weeks ago (in September or October 2017). It was about 2:00 pm or 3:00 pm.

I was with a friend. I was leaning down on a footbridge, she was above me. I looked up to speak to her and in the sky I saw a cigar-shaped object above the tops of the hills. It had no chem trail, no lights, no antennae, no legs, no windows, no sound. It was whitish gray. There was just the shape.

It moved across the horizon heading to the southeast, toward Madison and Chicago.

It is my hunch that it was not aliens but rather

evidence of the secret human space program.

A repeat from last year from the same man who took the photo printed this year. The same object he saw earlier, but photographed this year:

2018 UFO EVENTS

Art Bell, long-time radio host of the Coast to Coast Show dies on April 13, 2018 (June 17, 1945–April 13, 2018).

December 11, 2018, an object was spotted at about 1:05 pm on a beach in Marquette, Michigan, at a location well known for UFO sightings.

Local Sightings

A Woman from Viroqua

This happened on 7/22/17. I parked on County Road P in Marshland, Trempealeau County, just north of the Trempealeau Wildlife Refuge. I was sitting in my car watching lightning flash to the north and fireflies signal over the marsh in front of me. Around 9:45 pm, just when I decided to go, a white light appeared above the marsh. It was brighter than a star, brighter than headlights, and lower than a plane. It didn't have any green or red lights like a plane or drone would. It moved very slowly from my right to left at a constant height from the ground. From what I could tell, it was silent. At times it appeared to pause, and I had the feeling it was looking at me. I wanted to leave, but I thought I should wait and keep watching as the light moved northward. After about 15 more minutes, I left. Much later, I went back to the same spot during the daytime to see if there was a road at that elevation that I'd missed—maybe the light was from a vehicle. But there was nothing above the marsh, not even a hill in the distance where a road could have been.

Here is a report from Milwaukee of about the same time posted on the NUFORC website (National UFO Reporting Center):

Occurred: 7/16/2017 21:45 (Entered as 07/16/2017 21:45)
Reported: 7/17/2017 2:42:16 pm 14:42
Posted: 7/23/2017
Location: Milwaukee, WI
Shape: Light
Duration: 5 minutes
Given that local weather forecasts mentioned that the Aurora Borealis could be viewed in my area from around 10 pm, I went outside to see if they were, indeed, visible in Milwaukee. Unfortunately, they weren't.

However, while scanning the night sky around 9:45 pm, I noticed a light directly overhead. At first, I thought it was a satellite moving quietly, steadily due north. But then I saw it was blinking on and off in one-second intervals. No navigation lights were evident, and the light was not the strobe of a high-flying aircraft. In fact, two such high-flying jets (headed west) crossed well in front of this object, so it was easy to discern and compare what a strobe looked like at altitude vis-a-vis the unknown object.

In terms of illumination, the object/light resembled Saturn in both brightness and magnitude, although the quality of its light was a steady pale white while lit. Their light definitely wasn't a flash like that of a strobe, and it wasn't like the brilliant reflected light of a planet like Jupiter or Saturn. It had no star-like characteristics, either.

Unlike transient satellite flashes, the pulsing remained constant throughout the sighting. And, unlike a satellite, the object appeared to stop about 30 degrees above the horizon for 15-20 seconds, before heading off in a more northwest direction (a deviation under 10 degrees). It pulsed steadily until it disappeared from view. No navigation lights were ever in evidence; no contrail; no sound; no silhouette visible against the sky.

The sighting lasted about five minutes.

A Woman from Viola

I saw a lot of UFOs when I was growing up on the farm near Readstown. They would fly low while my sister and I would be sledding in the Winter. We would either run to the house or to the barn where Mom and Dad were milking the cows. I know of one other incident that I hear about but I'm not at liberty to talk about it. But it was scary. Some were oblong and then some were round. They were high up, enough that you could not see. They would stop and then fly off as quickly as they came.

They were so prevalent in the 50s. In the 1990s, I used to see them when I would drive back to Janesville from Beloit. It was so scary when they would stop and hover over you.

A Man from Westby

I was coming home and a huge red light was flashing right beside Highway 14, treetop level. I could see a shield around part of the light and the light was flashing. I practically drove right under it. I had to look right through my windshield to see the light. But as it flashed I noticed it wasn't lighting up the trees and once I got past it I couldn't see it anymore. But it didn't make a sound because I rolled down the window a little because I thought it might have been a helicopter but it wasn't.

2019 UFO EVENTS

Death of Stanton T. Friedman (July 29, 1934-May 13, 2019)

The first time I ever spoke on the phone with Stanton T. Friedman, he brought up the fact that he had worked on a secret government/aviation industry project which would have led to the development of an atomic airplane. I had never heard of this project and frankly, I was so rattled by the concept of a nuclear reactor flying over our heads that I could not help but blurt out: "atomic airplane?!", in the same tone of voice one might use to say: "rabies flavored candy!?". Friedman immediately replied: "That is precisely the attitude that destroyed that project." And I guess he was right. Friedman was a blunt, matter of fact science guy.

He got into UFOs as a topic for talks given to first scientific audiences and later the general public. He found that there was an interest in them and in time he became focused on the level of cover-up and government secrecy in the topic. He readily admitted that he had never seen a UFO himself, but that did not matter. The important thing for Stanton Friedman was the study of the thing—as an aviation topic, as a government topic. He readily said that the UFO issue was a "cosmic Watergate"—in reference to the government cover-up scandal of the 1970s.

One of his lectures on UFOs in Louisiana led him to meet Jesse Marcel, the initial military investigator of the Roswell incident. Marcel, was living in retirement in Houma, Louisiana, and a radio broadcaster in the audience of one of Friedman's talks there told him he ought to contact him. That indeed happened and the result was the beginning of the Roswell cottage industry. Friedman became the first civilian to locate the spot of the Roswell crash and wrote numerous books on the subject.

He told a committee of Congress that he believed that Earth is being visited by intelligently controlled extraterrestrial vehicles. He also believed that UFO sightings were consistent with magnetohydrodynamic propulsion.

Friedman earned a BS and MS from the University of Chicago in nuclear physics and worked for fourteen years for companies such as General Electric, Aerojet General Nucleonics, General Motors, and McDonnell Douglas. He died of a heart attack at the Toronto Pearson Airport.

Local Sightings

A Woman from Readstown

Turning off Hwy 14 onto 131 through town at 9:23 on the Cheapo Depot clock, there was a large red light in the NNW sky. The apparent altitude was hundreds not thousands, of feet above the hills. I said:

"What is that in the sky?" And again, "What IS that in

the sky?" Jane jokingly replied "UFO." Lost sight of it momentarily behind a tree and when it reappeared it was much farther away, could have been mistaken for a planet. or star. Was still clearly red, and I thought maybe Mars. (Not sure the location of Mars in the sky last night, though what I've looked up looks like more west.) Then it disappeared. After a few moments Jane said "There it is again." and then that it was gone again. I never did see it after the first time it vanished. Jane said that when she saw it the second time it still appeared red, but smaller than the first time we saw it.

A Woman from Viola:

We watched it for over an hour with binoculars.

First off, the grandson noticed it as a star in the daylight and that was a little before I messaged you. We got binocs cuz there just ain't no stars in the daylight.

It was round—almost looked like a translucent bubble. The outer rim reflected the sun—looked whiteish. At about the 6 o'clock position on the object, there was a white spot that moved back and forth from the 10 o'clock position to the 3 o'clock position, and at one point the white spot dropped below the bubble and moved back to the 3 o'clock position as if it turned. Like the sunset, the object turned orange. It looked to elongate as it moved further away. We lost sight of it with the naked eye long before Loren lost sight in the binocs—and that was probably 8:00 or 8:30 pm. We used the SKYVIEW app on Loren's phone to try to identify it but nothing registered. The Hubble and the ISS were on the other side of the Earth.

To give you an idea of distance, two passenger

airplanes flew underneath it and still had good size to be able to see with the naked eye.

One more thing...it looked more like a donut as you could see the blue sky behind it, so maybe bubble wasn't the right description.

A Man from Westby

I'm not sure if you call this a UFO experience or not. You decide. One night coming home from the river, I was coming up County K and at the top of the hill, I saw a bright white flashing light in the middle of the field. A couple of seconds later I found myself about five miles from where I should have been. I couldn't figure out how I got from point A to point C without going through point B. This is the second time this has happened on that road. The first time was in 1986, I believe. I was coming home from the river and I just went from County K to County O. The next thing I knew, I came to a stop sign. I couldn't figure out where there was a stop sign on County O, except where it meets Highway 56. Then I realized that that was where I was! So how did I go from the intersection of K/O to just outside of Viroqua? I didn't have any missing time either. This has haunted me ever since. And it was around 6 pm.

Reports from the National UFO Reporting Center Website (NUFORC)

A Report from LaFarge
Occurred: 4/5/2019 23:00 (Entered as 04/05/19 23:00)
Reported: 4/7/2019 7:55:40 am 07:55
Posted: 4/8/2019
Location: La Farge, WI

Shape: Formation

Duration: 4 minutes

3 lights separated like so. - - - Spaced and flying very fast above the reserve then appeared to cloak, with one light still showing...also a possibility of the object flying farther into the atmosphere. Flew across the horizon. No sound.

A Report from Prairie du Chien

Occurred: 6/10/2019 22:40 (Entered as 06/10/19 22:40)

Reported: 6/10/2019 8:51:55 pm 20:51

Posted: 6/20/2019

Location: Prairie du Chien, WI

Shape: Flash

Duration: 5 minutes

Bright flashes moving across the sky, in a Northwest direction. Random frequency of flash and brightness. Dogs responded as well.

A Report from Richland Center

Occurred: 8/7/2019 00:44 (Entered as 8/07/19 0:44)

Reported: 8/8/2019 2:55:44 pm 14:55

Posted: 8/23/2019

Location: Richland Center, WI

Shape: Light

Duration: 4-5 hours

Electromagnetic fields????!!!!

We have several sets of large windows in our bedroom and we are located around 1100 feet up on a Ridge. During early hours of the night on 8/7 into 8/8 bright lights kept shining through the curtains into our bedroom. At first, I thought it was traffic going by but after it kept waking me up, I stood up and opened the curtains to see where it was coming from which is when I found out it was coming from my son's car outside in our driveway. His car lights kept turning on and then off sometimes it only lasted a couple of seconds and sometimes quickly flashed on and off. As I looked to the south west I could see behind the tree line a moving blue red and white light.

My husband woke up to ask what that was all about and I told him and luckily the lights like a craft and then on the car lights again so I sent husband down to see if our son was doing something with his car but my husband went outside and looked around the house and found our son sleeping so he didn't want t to wake him up to ask him. This morning I ask my son if he was doing something with his car last night and he said no and I asked him if he was maybe rolling over on the key fab and he said no the key fabs battery was dead. This flashing on and off of car lights happened several times during the night so I didn't sleep much there was nothing else I didn't get up and keep checking outside like I wish I would've but my husband gets very irritated when I wake him up but I believe he was even spooked by this incident. Altogether there were three lighted moving objects spotted that were lit up in the sky no other which seemed very close and very bright there were no other stars in the sky it was cloudy. We've had several sightings out here before but nothing like this

Two Reports from Sparta
Occurred: 9/4/2019 20:30 (Entered as: 09/04/19 20:30)
Reported: 9/4/2019 7:25:21 PM 19:25

Posted: 9/6/2019
Location: Sparta, WI
Shape: Formation
Duration:7 minutes

Seen two orange lights moving together. Then one went dark and then the next one went dark. Then a group of four showed up and moved together before all going dark. I heard no noise.

Occurred: 9/4/2019 23:30 (Entered as 09/04/2019 23:30)
Reported: 9/4/2019 11:27:02 pm 23:27
Posted: 9/6/2019
Location: Sparta, WI
Shape: Sphere
Duration: 10 minutes

7 orbs-spheres east of fort McCoy, they just started disappearing one by one.

I was walking to the east and I started to see orange orbs-spheres? I started to walk faster and they started to disappear one by one. Ft. McCoy is down the road, so I thought it might be a military drill? Maybe not though. this is the third sighting I've had in my life so I do believe

2020 UFO EVENTS

The whole topic of UFOs or flying saucers hit a whole new level of credibility in the world press with the gray lady of New York journalism, the *New York Times* publishing a serious account of the U.S. Navy program to study the increasing problem of mysterious objects hanging around our ships and planes. In the case of the latter, there have been numerous instances of small and mid-sized objects flying extremely close to Navy jets:

From the *New York Times*, May 14, 2020:

"Navy fighter pilots reported close encounters with unidentified aerial vehicles, including several dangerously close, in eight incidents between June 27, 2013, and Feb. 13, 2019, according to documents recently released by the Navy.

"Two happened on one day, according to one of eight unclassified Navy safety reports released in response to requests filed under the Freedom of Information Act by news outlets, including *The New York Times*.

"Last month the Defense Department authenticated

three videos of aerial encounters previously published by *The Times*, accompanying accounts of Navy pilots who reported such close encounters."

Local Sightings

A Woman from Ferryville (recording)
Woman: "So, Dad, back when we were kids, I think I was probably 12 or 13. We were coming home—"

Man: "It was in '76..."

Woman: "Okay I was 16 then. Older than I remembered. So, what did we see? No one believes my version. I told them that your version was even more detailed."

Man: "We were going up Highway B, outside of Ferryville. It was in the mid to late afternoon. Up over a rise in the road, there was a flying saucer, right above the road. Just sitting there."

Woman: "So what were the details that you remember of what we saw."

Man: "I remember it sitting there. I could see windows in it. I was that close to see some round windows in it. I couldn't see nothing through the windows. I paid real close attention because I wanted to remember it."

Woman: "Unnhmmm."

Man: "And, uh, there was windows in it. And all of a sudden it took off, didn't make any noise. Didn't make any sound, (makes whoshing sound with lips). Nothing like that. It just took off...quiet. And, uh, flew out of the valley. And it had to be going a couple thousand miles an hour. Going so fast, it was a blur. Once it got going it was a blur. You couldn't see it."

Woman: "Well, I remember, I tell the kids, that it was sitting about the road... See if I'm wrong."

Man: "Okay."

Woman: "And I thought I remembered it picking up after a little bit."

Man: "It may have, yes."

Woman: "And when it disappeared it kind of made like a not a zig-zag but kind of an S pattern. And then it just took off. And it was gone in like one point five seconds."

Man: "Oh it was real fast."

Woman: "It was just gone."

Man: "If you didn't know it was there then you wouldn't know it. Because you couldn't see it once it got going. You couldn't see it anymore. It was just a blur."

Woman: "It went to the horizon, which would have been what, ten miles?"

Man: "It headed toward Rush Creek. I suppose you could see then miles from there. And it did that ten miles in like...a second."

Woman: "Ya, that is what I was thinking. I think that is really a fond memory at least of those of us in the front see that saw it."

Man: "Ya."

A Man from Readstown

My sighting of a UFO happened in Jan. or Feb. of 2018. I was on my way to visit the Tomah VA at about 6:30 am. About a mile North of Readstown on HWY 131 before reaching the Manning bridge. I saw a strange light just above the tree line on the Western hill roughly between Halverson and Jacobson property. Slowing down to see better I observed the light about a mile or more away that was yellow in color. I would size this with an HP Sodium light on a building probably a block away for comparison. The light had no sharp features or edges but could be compared kind of football shape and was moving slowly N/E, it had no blinking lights as an aircraft would. This stayed visible most of the way to Viola but was last clearly seen just near the salvage yard above the West hill. When I turned the sharp corner by KHS, it should have been in full view but as I slowed nearly to a stop it had disappeared. In less than 500 yards it was gone just like it had slipped into a crack between the Universe. How, I don't have a clue.

A Woman from Readstown

My son saw what he thought was a drone or a spaceship of some kind over a field

Next to Day Creek in Readstown. This was on September 16, 2020, at about 10:30 pm. It had blinking lights of various colors. It lit up the sky. It was not very far off the ground at first, but then suddenly it shot up in the sky away from me. The lights were still blinking. It kept going higher and higher. . He ran quickly into the house to tell me about it before it disappeared.

From National UFO Reporting Center
Occurred: 9/3/2020 21:15 (Entered as 09/03/20 21:15)
Reported: 9/3/2020 8:14:15 pm 20:14
Posted: 9/4/2020
Location: Mukwonago, WI
Shape: Triangle
Duration: 2 minutes

Triangle with 3 white lights on corners.

Occurred: 9/2/2020 20:40 (Entered as 09/03/2020 20:40)
Reported: 9/3/2020 12:55:57 pm 12:55
Posted: 9/4/2020
Location: Indianford/Fulton/Edgerton, WI
Shape: Triangle
Duration: 45-60 seconds.

4 large white lights with 2 on either side (cross-shaped) surrounded by 3 larger red lights on top, left, and right side

Night fishing at Indianford, left about 8:30. Noticed a strange light (Strobing) hovering about 125 feet off the ground in distance. We left going that direction. As we turned south onto Hwy 51 we noticed it was near a com. tower—whose red lights mysteriously were not on anymore? As we approached the area we could see clearly it was hovering—NOT moving. Whatsoever. Got underneath it, still not moving, and not making a single sound. that's when we saw it closer than comfort. I wanted to slam on my brakes but was paralyzed, there were 3 drivers behind me that HAD to have seen this. My fiancé was screaming to pull over, by the time I drove 500 ft to turn around, cleared the trees it was about a mile away, almost still visible - and then it was 100 miles North, just a light that eventually disappeared. Did not get a clear photo. If I would have pulled over immediately—the photo evidence would have been unbelievable.

Occurred: 8/4/2020 03:00 (Entered as 08/04/20 03:00)
Reported: 8/5/2020 7:28:14 am 07:28
Posted: 8/6/2020
Location: Madison, WI
Shape: Triangle
Duration: 1.5 hours

Large triangle object/craft emitting extremely bright light and deploying smaller lights/ objects

This sighting took place over two nights/ mornings starting on August 4th, 2020.

August 4th, 2020- 0300 hours: I witnessed a large in scale object in the sky in a Northeast position above the State Capitol building in downtown Madison Wisconsin. It was emitting an extremely bright white light that was almost difficult to stare at due to its intensity. The object in question was mostly stationary in the sky only varying a pattern of clockwise movement in a minute fashion and was slowly rotating on its axis. It was roughly 30 to 40,000 feet in altitude, and in comparison to cargo jets flying nearby, it was determined to be at least 4 to 5 times the size of a large jumbo jet (example being an Airbus A380).

The object in question was not a satellite or the ISS due to its size, placement within the atmosphere/ sky, and contradiction to the ISS flight path per NASA source.

0330: I witnessed several small lights/ lighted objects dart out of the primary object in question, they flew out in all directions toward the horizon. The object maintained a super-vibrant light emission and proximity to the aforementioned.

0400: The object began to slowly move upward in the sky and diminish in size as if moving out of the atmosphere. Just after dawn broke it was gone.

August 5th, 2020—0300: The object in question returned, but at a much higher altitude/ further distance than the prior night, it again maintained a somewhat fixed position for a period of time though was rotating on axis more. I maintained observation as able while performing work duties.

0330: I observed the object in question intensify and diminish its light projection, and begin to move to higher altitude/ outward toward the atmosphere, then back to the previous altitude.

0400: I observed several of the smaller lights/ objects move from west to east under the primary large craft in question, then spontaneously disappear just low and east of the large object. The large object had maintained the high-intensity light emission once again.

0430: The large object in question once again moved upward and outward at a moderate consistent pace out of the atmosphere until it had disappeared from physical view right around dawn breaking.

End of Report.

Same night in Dallas, Texas

Occurred: 8/4/2020 20:19 (Entered as 08/04/20 20:19)

Reported: 8/4/2020 9:31:13 pm 21:31

Posted: 8/6/2020

Location: Dallas, TX

Shape: Cigar

Duration: ~20 minutes

Lone massive object in the sky

At first, I thought it was a plane leaving a trail, but this was going from up to down in direction. At first, it left a bit of a trial but then it was just a massive long shape. It looked white from the distance I was at. Sky was completely clear; this was the ONLY object in the sky. WAY bigger than a plane. Could not have been aircraft, I live by both DFW and Dallas Love Field, I see many planes daily.

An Identified Flying Object (they are not all flying saucers)
A friend from Texas:

About 1984 or so, I lived in Athens, Ga. My front yard was about 4 1/2 feet above street level and the house was at least that much above the yard. Looking out my back porch door, I could see a huge oak tree in my neighbor's yard to the left. My back yard was bordered in the rear by a privet hedge and a school and schoolyard behind it. To the right, I could see a slight uphill and all the way to downtown (about 2 1/2 miles.) Just right of it was the neighbor's garage and yard.

On a warm summer night, I stood in the back porch doorway, enjoying the cooler night air. I could hear a car pass on the road in front. Suddenly I noticed a light apparently just in front of my neighbor's tree. It had a trapezoid or pie pan shape, except that the sides had different angles. It moved to the right and diminished in size as if it were moving over to the schoolyard and then off to downtown. It had to be moving at increasing speed as it moved away. As it almost reached the horizon, it just blinked off.

I wondered if I really saw this. It was just light, but it seemed to be physically there. I could not place how, but I thought that something seemed suspicious.

I stood there, pondering the experience and it happened again. I noticed that the UFO suddenly appeared in front of the tree. It did not move to the tree. A car passed by in front of the house, again, just as before. It occurred to me that the movement as left to right, not taking in the distance perception, correlated to the auto passing in front of the house.

I concluded that there was a temperature inversion that reflected lights from the street to the rear window of a car parked on the street. The angle distorted the symmetry of that window. It first showed in front of the tree and moved, getting smaller as it moved along.

After recognizing this. I would stand in that doorway at nights with similar weather conditions to watch the show.

2021 UFO EVENTS

The *New Yorker* magazine publishes a long article about the UFO phenomenon, a topic unprecedented for this highly esteemed, highly established literary publication.

Included in the 5,000-page stimulus bill is a mandate for the Department of Defense to release its UFO information. The deadline for this release is July, 2021.

Luis Elisondo, the former Pentagon officer in charge of the UFO research program called Advanced Aerospace Technology Identification Program (or ATTIP) believes that there are five characteristics called "Unique Observables" which effectively identify UFOs worth study:

"These characteristics include; instantaneous acceleration, hypersonic velocity, low observability, trans medium travel (the ability to operate in various environments), and positive lift, in which you have vehicles that can fly without the apparent need for control surfaces, wings, or even engines."

In the past year, Elisondo has been appearing on all

manner of media, discussing UFOs and the 2004 aircraft films of "Tic-Tac" like objects by the U.S. Navy in 2004.

The long awaited report by the Director of the National Unidentified Aerial Phenomenon Task Force was released at the end of June. Those people who were hoping that the report would verify the existence of entities from outer space were disappointed. The report in fact made no direct reference to ETs:

'Our analysis of the data supports the construct that if and when individual UAP incidents are resolved they will fall into one of five potential explanatory categories: airborne clutter, natural atmospheric phenomena, USG or U.S. industry developmental programs, foreign adversary systems, and a catchall "other" bin.'

"Other" perhaps could allude to off-Earth visitors, but the report said more science and higher budgets would be necessary to probe that category.

Local Sightings

Sighting from NUFORC
Occurred: 1/9/2021 06:00 (Entered as 1-9-2021 6:00)
Reported: 1/9/2021 8:08:32 pm 20:08
Posted: 1/19/2021
Location: Athelstane, WI
Shape: Disk
Duration: 3 minutes

"Came out the back door & immediately noticed top hat-shaped craft with amber & red lights and moving away from me towards the city, first spotted when seen over pine ridge motocross track, grabbed binoculars &

looked at it for 10 seconds & just faded out and was the size of a football field. Huge!"

Line of UFOs (NUFORC)
Occurred : 12/5/2020 19:00 (Entered as 12/05/2030 19:00)
Reported: 12/4/2020 5:23:12 pm 17:23
Posted: 12/23/2020
Location: Whitewater, WI
Shape: Formation
Duration: 1 minute. Straight linear formation of about 100 solid lights that went out one by one

Driving into Whitewater from the north on Highway 59. Passenger spotted a straight linear formation of bright solid lights out the window towards the city and rolled down the window to attempt a photo. I only saw about 20 because I was driving, however, he claims to have witnessed close to 100. Turning off the road we witnessed the lights go out one by one. The total event took place over the course of about a minute and we did not see them again.

UFO BOOK REVIEW

Kaela Firebaugh has written a review of a novel I have just written that deals with local history and the UFO topic:

Book Review by Kaela Firebaugh
No Place to Go by John H. Sime. Published by Lovstad in 2015. 151 pages.

Quite early in *No Place to Go,* an engaging gem of a book by local Readstown author John Sime, readers realize they are in for a wild and unpredictable ride. While clearly paying homage to the classic detective novel, Sime blends in elements of historical and science fiction to create a unique and intriguing tale.

Anyone familiar with the SW Wisconsin area from Madison to La Crosse will delight in Sime's choice of locales for this richly described, nostalgic 1950's era novel. Whether invoking a vivid picture of the historic La Crosse County courthouse, Vernon County's round barns, or the décor and denizens of the numerous dive bars in the area,

Sime tells a thoroughly local tale with a keen eye for detail.

Cy Butt, a rumpled, hard drinking lawyer and practical joker, "known in every bar within a hundred miles of Viroqua" is the strangely appealing central character. From Butt's cramped room in the Hotel Fortney to his hat from Felix's Clothing Store, Sime has created a personally flawed but charming Viroquan hero. After decades as a professional student at University of Madison, Cy is working as a lawyer and joins forces with the Wisconsin Attorney General as a secret investigator to solve a series of disturbing unsolved crimes. Cy enlists support from an eclectic cast of characters—including a few from his days at the University—like the eccentric Professor R. M. Alterweise: a five-foot-tall scholar and mystic who alerts Cy to the "evil cabal...who have operated a secret cult here in the heart of Madison for decades!"

Although it is filled with wonderfully detailed settings and richly imagined characters, *No Place to Go* becomes a classic page turner as Cy and company are drawn deeper into the realm of the mysterious cult, with its evil, ageless "Master" and heartless, murderous henchmen. There is plenty of intrigue, which is given an extra jolt by an overarching conspiracy involving extra-terrestrials. I would recommend this book to anyone, but especially to the readership of the *Epitaph-News*. The story alone is worthy, but the local setting and historical basis makes this book special and fun to read.

A WISCONSIN UFO CHRONOLOGY WITH SIDELIGHTS IN OTHER PLACES

(Partly taken from Richard W. Heiden's "UFO Report from Wisconsin"; prepared for the Center for UFO Studies, Also partly taken from famous accounts of events worldwide)

April 11, 1897—UFO seen in downtown Milwaukee by thousands of people.

April 17, 1897—Alleged crash of a UFO in Aurora, Texas; with occupant supposedly buried in local cemetery.

July 1941—Alleged crash of UFO near Cape Girardeau, Missouri; wreckage retrieved, with occupants.

June 3-4, 1942—Green Bay, Wisconsin; UFO takes control of car.

June 24, 1947—1947—Mt. Rainier, Wash.; Kenneth Arnold

sees crescent-like object from his plane and which the press likens to a saucer skimming across water when thrown. This inspired the term "Flying Saucer". Arnold himself said it had a crescent or chevron shape.

July 4, 1947—Roswell, New Mexico; Crash of UFO with wreckage retrieved, with occupants.

August 19, 1947—Polonia, Wisconsin; 9:30 pm; UFO seen by 8 people.

Fall; 1947—Mequon, Wis.; "flying white cigar" seen by boy.

April 18, 1961—Eagle River, Wis.; Joe Simonton sees UFO land and encounters occupants who give him pancakes produced in their craft.

Late Sept. 1961—New Hampshire; Betty and Barney Hill abducted by ETs. Later documented as book *The Interrupted Journey: Two Hours Aboard a UFO* by John Fuller and filmed as *The UFO Incident.*

Oct. 14, 1973—Phantom Lakes, Wis.; UFO.

Oct. 18, 1973-Lomira, Wis.; UFO.

Nov. 29, 1973—Jacksonport, Wis.; UFO.

Nov. 5, 1975—White Mts., Arizona; Travis Walton abducted by ETs (as depicted in the film *Fire in the Sky*).

April 22, 1976—Elmwood, Wis.; Deputy sees UFO.

Aug. 16, 1976—Peninsula State Park, Door County, Wis.; 4:00 am, UFO and ET contact.

Aug. 23, 1976—Peninsula State Park, Door County, Wis.; 4:15 am, UFO and ET contact.

Nov. 4, 1977—Hubertus, Wis.; 2:30 pm; UFO lands and grass on that spot won't grow later on.

Dec. 1977—Dodge County, Wis.; Photo taken of UFO.

March 22, 1978—8:45 pm to 9:15 pm; UFO traced from

Cumberland, Wis. to St. Paul, Minn.

April 19, 1978—Colfax, Wis; Photo taken of UFO by police officer.

May 25, 1978—Park Falls, Wis.; UFO.

May 30, 1978—New Berlin, Wis.; UFO.

June 17, 1978—Coloma, Wis.; 10:57 pm; UFO.

June 24, 1978—Evansville, Wis. to New Lisbon, Wis; 10:48 pm to 11:50 pm UFO seen by pilot and radar.

June 26, 1978—Menasha, Wis.; 11 pm; UFO.

July 6, 1978—Kenosha, Wis.; 10:17 pm; UFO.

July 28, 1978—Lake Michigan (Sturgeon Bay, Wis., Milwaukee, among other ports); UFO seen from approximately 8 pm to midnight.

July 28-29, 1978—Two Rivers, Wis.; 11:30 pm; Photos taken of UFO.

July 29, 1978—Apostle Islands, Wis.; 2:40 am; UFO.

Aug. 1, 1978 —Waldo, Wis.; UFO.

Aug. 9, 1978—Sturgeon Bay, Wis.; UFO.

Aug. 9, 1978—Two Rivers, Wis.; UFO.

Aug. 13, 1978—Menasha, Wis.; 10:00 pm; Photo taken of UFO.

Aug. 13, 1978—Brookfield, Wis.; 11:20 pm; Two policemen witness UFO.

Aug. 14, 1978—Merrill, Wis.; 1:35 am; UFO.

Aug. 20, 1978—Shawano, Wis.; UFO.

Aug. 26, 1978—Spooner, Wis.; UFO "traces" found, later identified as "fungus spores".

September 6, 1978—Prairie du Chien, Wis., McGregor and Monona, Iowa; 8:45 pm to 10:15 pm. Dozens of witnesses report UFO.

September 10, 1978—Fond cu Lac, Wis.; 11:45 pm; UFO.

September 29, 1978—Cross Plains, Wis.; 8:15 pm; UFO.

October 21, 1978—Melbourne, Australia; 7:06 pm; Pilot Frederick Valentich disappears while reporting a UFO over the radio of his plane.

Nov. 21, 1978—Bayfield, Wis.; UFOs.

Nov. 30, 1978—Monroe, Wis.; UFO.

Dec. 5, 1978—Price County, Wis.; 3:40; Photo taken of UFO.

December 21 to December 30, 1978—Christchurch, New Zealand; UFOs tracked by radar and filmed by television camera.

Dec. 27, 1978—Marathon County, Wis.; 6:15 pm; UFO.

April 21, 1979—River Falls, Wis.; UFOs.

Aug. 25, 1979—Hudson, Wis.; 4 witnesses to UFO.

Aug. 29, 1979—Balsam Lake, Wis; 3 witnesses to UFO.

Sept. 1, 1979—New Glarus, Wis.; 3 deputies witness UFO.

Sept. 3, 1979—Balsam Lake, Wis.; 2 couples witness UFO.

Sept. 4, 1979—New Richmond, Wis.; 5 witnesses to UFO.

Sept. 4, 1979—Dresser, Wis.; 5 witnesses to UFO.

Sept. 6, 1979—LaFarge, Wis.; Several witnesses see disc-shaped, multicolored UFOs on two different occasions; with two Vernon County Deputies among the witnesses. They contact a nearby radar facility and are told: "Don't worry about it." As reported in the *La Crosse Tribune*, Sept. 7, 1979, the deputies said they saw nothing and the La Crosse FAA said they saw nothing unusual in the skies.

Sept. 7, 1979—South Milwaukee, Wis.; 8:30 pm; UFO.

Sept. 15, 1979—Waukesha County, Wis.; 4:00 am; UFO.

Sept. 20, 1979—Fennimore, Wis.; 5:30 am; UFO.

Sept. 20, 1979—Monroe, Wis.; 6:00 am; UFOs sighted by several drivers.

June 13, 1980—Northwest Wisconsin; 6 to 8 pm; Numerous reports of UFOs in Menomonie, Bloomer, and Grantsburg areas.

Jan. 15, 1980—Elm Grove, Wis.; 10:30 pm; 3 witnesses to UFO.

Jan. 16, 1980—Elm Grove, Wis.; 5:45 am; 3 witnesses to UFO.

1980s—Elmwood, Wis.; So many UFO sightings occur in this area that a local group will set up a "UFO Landing Strip", and in July 1988, two agents from the Central Intelligence Agency's Domestic Collection Division will be sent there to study the phenomenon (*Out There*; Howard Blum; Pocket Books; 1990; pg. 166).

Aug. 30 or 31, 1980—Marinette County, Wis.; 9:30 pm; "Red ball with a cone-shaped red light going about it" seen by witness with binoculars (Heiden, pg. 21). (see sighting #IV A1, 1993 article)

March 1981—Milwaukee; "Boy and brother saw something like a tower formation of flashing lights stationary; 3 to 4 minutes duration". (Heiden pg. 13) (see sighting #IV A1, 1993 article).

November, 1981—Madison, Wis.; 11:00 pm: woman reports a black triangular UFO.

March, 1982—Readstown, Wis.; 4:00 P.M; Man sees daylight disc do 90 degree turn and head east over Highway 14.

April 2, 1986—Upstate New York; Author Whitley Strieber and son meet ETs in an experience documented in book and film *Communion*.

March 20, 1988—Richland County, Wis.; Prof. John Salter and son meet ETs at dusk on hilltop field just off Highway 14.

February 1993—Dodge County, Wis.; UFOs reported.

March 9, 1993—Kenosha, Wisconsin; 11:00 pm; Woman reports UFO "as large as 9 houses." (see sighting #IV A1, 1993 article).

July 28, 1993—Oconomowoc, Wis.; 12:30 pm;

A WRONG TURN INTO DESTINY IN READSTOWN

On March 20, 1988, Rev. Jesse Jackson won the Michigan Democratic caucuses. Also, Soviet Foreign Minister Eduard Shevardnadze and Secretary of State George Shultz met in Washington, D.C. to discuss the upcoming summit meeting between Gorbachev and Reagan. And, a man from Grand Forks, North Dakota, driving a 1987 Ford pickup truck made a wrong turn in Readstown while traveling east on U.S. Highway 14. Rather than turning south onto U.S. Highway 61 as they had intended, they kept going east. History might come to see that that wrong turn in Readstown was by far the most significant event to have occurred on that day in this country, on this planet, in this universe.

Prof. John Salter, Jr. of the University of North Dakota at Grand Forks and his almost twenty-three-year-old son, John III, were traveling to New Orleans to attend the

Popular Culture Association/American Culture Association convention. He was to deliver a paper entitled "Civil Rights and Self Defense" before that group. A professor in the University of North Dakota's Department of American Indian Studies (and department chairman), Salter had been an activist in the 1960s Southern Civil Rights Movement. He is the author of Jackson, Mississippi: An American Chronicle of Struggle and Schism, which records that era. For some reason, Salter decided to go to New Orleans via Southwest Wisconsin.

Two-lane U.S. Highways 14/61 hardly make the most logical route from North Dakota to New Orleans. However, Prof. Salter and his son, for some reason, found themselves drawn in this direction of this road. As he looked back upon it, Salter found himself motivated by an odd wave of nostalgia for Cedar Rapids, Iowa (he had taught at Coe College in Cedar Rapids from 1968 to 1969). This nostalgia was stimulated by a children's song often sung by Salter and his then young family at that time and at that place—*Kookaburra*, an Australian lullaby:

> "Kookaburra sits in the old gum tree.
> Merry, merry king of the bush is he.
> Laugh, Kookaburra, laugh Kookaburra.
> Gay your life must be!"

The more that Salter remembered this song, the more he seemed to be drawn to Highway 61 as a means of avoiding Cedar Rapids and its cloying sentimental attachments. And since this is almost like a vacation, why not? This was evidently not a conscious decision reached by Salter and his son, they simply got to La Crosse in the late afternoon, ate, gassed up, and headed southeast on Highway 14/61. The last thing they remembered, they had reached the top of Ten Mile or West Coon Valley Hill. They had just passed the wayside at the La Crosse/ Vernon Counties line. The next thing they knew, they were climbing the Bashford Hill in Richland County, going east on Highway 14, just at the west end of the short four-lane stretch outside of Richland Center. Now it was past sunset. They noticed that it was 6:25 pm. Both men again dropped into amnesia. The next thing they knew, it was 7:45 pm, they were now heading down County ZZ for Highway 14, at the top of the Bashford Hill. They turned right onto Highway 14 and headed toward Richland Center. Again, "a curtain of amnesia descended", until they found themselves east of Richland Center, at the intersection of U.S. 14 and Wis. 58. Here, they consulted a map and found out that they had not only missed Readstown and their intended turn down Highway 61 for Dubuque, but they seemed to have "lost" several chunks of time. They continued on their journey, sleeping at Bettendorf, Iowa, and breakfasting in Peoria, Illinois.

The next morning, on the other side of Peoria, they saw "an incredibly bright object, glowing with an extraordinary shimmering silverness" moving in the sky toward and above their car. This was along a stretch of highway where they were the only vehicles to be seen.

"It was about two-thirds the size of the full double highway and, when about 200 yards from us, swerved slightly and rose over the pickup at an angle. We could now make out its saucer-like form, and I think, a slight dome." (page 8, *An Account of the Salter UFO Encounters of March*, 1988, by John R. Salter, Jr.; 1989).

Even as they saw the ship, the Salters seemed to believe that it was a friendly appearance done for just their benefit.

As the months went by, memories came back to both men of their missing time experiences. To date, neither man has been hypnotized. These memories have just come back as if some imposed forgetfulness had worn off:

"Invariably, as they've developed, my recall vignettes—images and segments—have come first as vivid dreams in the early morning hours, then recede back temporarily into unconsciousness before emerging the following late morning or afternoon as clear memory of the earlier dream or dreams." (Page 8, ibid).

This recall process occurred for both father and son, who were now separated by half a continent—as the son and his wife had moved to California. Both the father and the son gradually remembered the startling details of their drive down Highway 14/61 on March 20, 1988. On that day, both maintain, they had left Highway 14 on the other side of the Bashford Hill, turned right up into Pier Spring Road. They drove a ways up this narrow, woods enshrouded, gravel road. They stopped the truck, got out and met a group of humanoids (which was hidden in the woods a short walk away), and then they went back to the truck. They drove on up Pier Spring Road, turned right onto County ZZ, which swung them back around to Highway 14.

Since that day, UFOs (Unidentified Flying Objects) have been a big part of the life of Prof. Salter. He now teaches a course at the University of North Dakota Department of Indian Studies called IS 379: *UFOs, ETs, and Close Encounters*. Over 170 students enrolled in this course for fall 1991, more would have signed up if a bigger room had been available. Students of about sixty majors were present—"right across the UND undergraduate dimension". Many of these students were from Aerospace Sciences.

Prof. Salter has returned to Western Wisconsin a number of times. The most recent visit was made in October 1991. The missing time episodes are all the more amazing since both he and his son went Coon Valley, Westby, Viroqua, and Readstown, and came away without the slightest memory of any of it. Salter and his daughter took the same journey in June 1989:

"In the June, 1989 junket, I saw nothing beyond the large hill that I recognized. (Editor's Note: This is evidently the Ten Mile or Coon Valley Hill)—everything was "new"— even though there were quaint towns, unique hill formations, and Indian and other place names that could have definitely registered. (In checking with John III, now in California, no landmarks that I indicated were remembered by him). Among other things, we did not recall Readstown and the much advertised forking of the roads with Highway 14 and 61 very conspicuously parting company." (page 5, ibid).

There were two types of humanoids met by Prof. Salter and his son on Pier Spring Road:

"Up closer, they are four to four and one-half feet tall, thin bodies and thin limbs—but comparatively large and quasi-slanted eyes. There are several of these people— perhaps six of seven—and a taller humanoid figure, almost as tall as I (six feet) and not as proportionately think as the others. His features are more, as we use the term, "human", —and he may well be a mixed blood."

(pages 12-13, ibid).

The communication between the Salters and the humanoids was telepathic. An implant was placed into Prof. Salter's right nostril by these individuals and they also gave him two injections of some kind. They also carefully scanned his son's face with some sort of "flashlight" type instrument whose head is so soft it melds into the contours of his face.

Later, as the tall humanoid escorted the Salters back to their truck, everyone seemed to have the feeling that things had gone very well for everyone. They all communicated: "will see one another again, in another place, in another time." As the Salters sat alone in the pickup, they watched the brightly lit UFO rise and fly off.

Both Salters feel that the whole thing was a very positive experience. They felt this way despite the fact that they believe themselves to have been the subjects of some sort of sophisticated mind control from the outset of their adventure.

"Their actions (motivations and effects and related factors) are quite positive. While I think it's possible that there may be some "experimentation" involved, I think this is ethically and honorably done—and to good ends. However, I believe the basic thrusts focus on helping some of us (directly) 'keep on keeping on' in the business of edging humanity closer and closer to the Sun (figuratively speaking) and sensitizing humanity with respect to the relatively nearby presence of other forms of intelligent life." (page 20, ibid).

They are convinced that whatever these visitors want, they mean us no harm. Since that time, Prof. Salter (and his son) have seen numerous medical changes in his own body. His hair and fingernails grow faster. His wounds heal more rapidly. He has effortlessly given up smoking, after a heavy 40-year habit (he was once a 4 pack a day cigarette smoker, later a pound per week pipe tobacco user). He has also recalled previous UFO encounters.

The tall humanoid indicated to Prof. Salter that their spacecraft originates from the Zeta Reticuli star system. This is a double-starred system, 37 light years away, in which the two suns are both dimmer than our own.

The Salter adventure was the subject of a CBS television documentary entitled Visitors from the Unknown. This was broadcast in May 1991 and will probably be rebroadcast soon.

Epitaph-News, January 16, 1992

<u>Sources</u>

Salter, John R., Jr. *An Account of the Salter UFO Encounters of March, 1988*; copyright 1989, John R. Salter, Jr.

Thanks to:
Terry Arbegust, John and Eldri Salter, and Gary Sime

EMBALMING E.T.:

A New Mexico practitioner's close encounter with a UFO and the Air Force

In the summer of 1947, Glenn Dennis was a font of information about embalming and embalming fluid, since he had just graduated from San Francisco Mortuary College. A lifelong

Roswell, New Mexico, resident, Mr. Dennis, today 68 years old, recalls that he began his 35 years in the funeral business by going to work for the local funeral director as a car washer, a "go-fer," and, eventually, an apprentice. Mr. Dennis eventually served as chairman of the New Mexico State Board of Funeral Directors and Embalmers for a time. It was during his tenure that New Mexico first required college study as a requirement for licensing in that state. Though just starting out in the business, Mr. Dennis might have been just the right person to answer the phone just after lunch on Tuesday, July 8, 1947, because an older practitioner, for whom the textbooks were a distant memory, would have been unable to answer the questions about embalming and embalming fluid, and the handling of deceased remains that the U.S. government asked Glenn Dennis that day.

When the phone at Ballard Funeral Home rang, Mr. Dennis found the mortuary officer at Roswell Army Air Base on the other end of the line: "This is just a hypothetical situation," he began. "But do you have any three-foot or four-foot-long, hermetically sealed caskets?"

"Yes, we have four feet," Glenn Dennis answered.

"How many do you have?"

"One."

"How soon before you could get more?"

"If we called the warehouse in Amarillo, Texas, Before 3 pm today, they can have them here tomorrow morning. Is there some kind of a problem?" Mr. Dennis asked.

The funeral home where he worked had the government contract with the base to handle deaths, including air crashes.

"No, this is just for our information."

The call ended. Mr. Dennis went back to work. About an hour later, the same mortuary officer called back.

"How do you handle bodies that have been exposed out in the desert for four or five days?" he asked, again assuring Glenn there was no crash. This was just a "hypothetical" situation. They were just gathering information for their files. The man also wanted to know what embalming fluid did to tissue, what embalming fluid was made of, what to do to close holes in bodies made by predators, how best to pick up such remains.

Glenn answered all questions, and his performance was no doubt impressive and a credit to his profession—right out of embalming school! Nevertheless, Glenn's curiosity was piqued.

"Just call us for a situation like that!" Mr. Dennis pointed out to the officer. "Is there some kind of crash?"

"No, no, just gathering information for our files."

Glenn's firm had handled up to 20 bodies at a time in crashes at the base. The firm had constructed an addition next to the embalming room just for those situations. About an hour after that strange call, an opportunity presented itself for a trip to the base. A young airman had injured his hand in a motorcycle accident. Now, Glenn was called upon in the capacity of his firm's ambulance service to transport this man back to base.

The airman was able to sit in the front seat of the hearse-ambulance with Glenn. The guards at the gate, familiar with Glenn, readily let the hearse through. Glenn was a familiar figure at the base—even being an honorary member of its Officers Club. He drove his ambulance to the base hospital and backed up to the loading area, as was his customary procedure. This time, however, he noted there were two field ambulances in the spot he preferred, so he parked next to them. He and the airman got out and started into the hospital.

As Glenn passed the field ambulances, which were guarded by an MP, he looked into the open back end. Inside both ambulances was an enormous amount of a silvery, metallic-like material, which seemed to be as thin as aluminum foil, but not as flexible. Glenn particularly noticed two chunks, each of which seemed to be between 3 feet and 2.5 feet high, and "curved like the bottom of a canoe."

Glenn also noticed odd markings, in some sort of "hieroglyphic-like" script that was totally unfamiliar. Mr. Dennis sauntered down the hall of the hospital, heading to a soda machine—as was customary after bringing in a patient. Here Glenn had a nasty encounter with an unfamiliar officer.

"Looks like you've got an air crash. Should I go back to town and get my equipment ready?" Glenn casually asked the officer he saw in the hallway.

"Who the hell are you?" was the response. Glenn introduced himself and explained his role in handling crash victims.

The response to this was an order to get out of the hospital and off the base.

Glenn gladly complied and turned to head back down the hall. He had not gone far when he heard someone scream after him. "Bring that (man) back here!" And two MPs appeared from somewhere, grabbed Glenn, and took him back to a red-haired officer.

"Now don't you go back to Roswell and start shooting off your mouth about how there's been a crash out here or..." A series of threats followed. Glenn said, "You can't talk to me like that. I'm a civilian. You haven't got any say over me."

"Listen, undertaker, somebody's gonna be picking your bones out of the sand." And the officer ordered the MPs to personally escort Glenn back to the funeral home, which they did. On the way down the hall, however, Mr. Dennis had an interesting encounter with a female nurse he knew. A door opened to a supply room as Glenn and the MPs went down the hallway. Out stepped the nurse, whom Glenn had dealt with at the hospital. She carried a towel over the lower part of her face. Glenn at first thought she had been crying.

"Glenn, what are you doing here? You're going to get shot!" she exclaimed.

"Well, I'm leaving." He pointed meaningfully to his armed escort. He noticed that the nurse was followed out of the supply room by two unfamiliar men, both of whom also had towels over their noses and mouths. Farther into the supply room Glenn noticed gurneys.

The next day, that same nurse called Glenn at the funeral home. The two of them arranged to meet at the Officers's Club. It was there that she unfolded for Glenn an extraordinary tale—a flying saucer had crashed out in the desert and the Army had recovered three dead aliens. Two of the bodies were badly mangled, both by the crash and by predators. One body was in fairly good condition. All the while, she kept becoming more and more emotional. Finally, she was openly crying in the club. Glenn thought it best to take her back to the nurses' quarters on base. After he dropped off the nurse, he never saw or heard from her again. His later inquiries produced the information that she was transferred to England. He obtained an address in England, wrote to her, and received back the letters, which were stamped "addressee deceased." He heard that she was killed in a plane crash.

Talking to Glenn that afternoon in the Officer's Club, the nurse provided anatomical details. She said that they were little, smaller than an adult human. She said that the hands were different, too, that they only had four fingers with the middle two protruding longer than the others. She saw no opposable thumb. She also said that the anatomy of the arm was different. The bone from the shoulder to the elbow was shorter than the bone from the elbow to the wrist. The heads were larger than a human's. The eyes were large and concave in shape. She said that all the features, the nose, and the ears, and the eyes were slightly concave.

The nurse went on to draw a small sketch of the alien bodies, using the back of a prescription paper. It showed that the bodies had four digits on each hand. The end of each digit consisted of a sort of pad. Mr. Dennis eventually lost this sketch but has reproduced his own version.

The nurse also stated that the two men following her out of the storage room were pathologists from Walter Reed hospital in Washington, D.C. The nurse explained the towels over their faces. "Until they got those bodies frozen, the smell was so bad you couldn't get within 100 feet of them without gagging." It was when the nurse stepped out of the room where she had been assisting two doctors on the bodies, to get some air, that she ran into Mr. Dennis.

She explained that even the doctors were getting sick, and the smell was so bad they had to turn off the air conditioning to keep it from spreading throughout the hospital. Soon, they gave up trying to work under such conditions and completed the preparation of the bodies in a hangar.

Stanton T. Friedman, a nuclear physicist who has written several books and many articles on UFOs, first brought the UFO crash at Roswell to the attention of the public. Since the late 1960s, Mr. Friedman, now 59 years old and a resident of New Brunswick, Canada, has been an active researcher, writer, and lecturer on UFOs. He has spoken at over 600 colleges in the United States, Canada, and Europe. He has been on numerous radio and television shows, such as Sally Jessie Raphael and Tom Snyder. He first heard about the Roswell incident while in Louisiana for a radio interview. Someone at the radio station told him about the late Jesse Marcel, who then lived in nearby Houma, LA.

Marcel told Mr. Friedman that he had been heavily involved in the initial retrieval of the wreckage and alien bodies at Roswell. This information spurred Mr. Friedman to investigate the incident and the result has been three books, numerous articles, and a 1989 NBC TV feature on *Unsolved Mysteries*. It was while he was in New Mexico to film that 1989 TV episode that Mr. Friedman first met Glenn Dennis.

Mr. Dennis did not seek out Mr. Friedman, but rather Mr. Friedman used his research skill to track him down. Mr. Friedman reasoned that there must have been professional mortuary knowledge used by someone if alien bodies were recovered. Therefore, he asked sources whether military or private morticians were used on the base in 1947. When told that private morticians were used, he found out who—and that led him to Glenn Dennis.

Mr. Dennis refused to appear of the "Unsolved Mysteries" show, but he was very willing to speak with Mr. Friedman.

Today, Mr. Dennis is involved with the UFO Museum

and Research Center in Roswell. This facility opened last year and has already been visited by more than 18,000 people. The center has numerous books, Research materials, and exhibit items.

Walter Haut, the 1957 press relations officer at Roswell Air Base, is also involved in the museum. It was Mr. Haut who released a press statement at about 11 a.m. on July 8, 1947:

"The many rumors regarding the flying discs became a reality yesterday when the intelligence office of the 509th Bomb Group of the Eighth Air Force, Roswell Army Air Field, was fortunate enough to gain possession of a disc through the cooperation of one of the local ranchers and the sheriff's office of Chaves County."

"The flying object landed on a ranch near Roswell sometime last week. Not having phone facilities, the rancher stored the disc until such time as he was able to contact the sheriff's office, who in turn notified Major Jesse A. Marcel of the 509th Bomb Group Intelligence Office."

"Action was immediately taken and the disc was picked up at the rancher's home. It was inspected at the Roswell Army Air Field and subsequently loaned by Major Marcel to higher headquarters."

Mr. Haut today maintains that he issued this statement at the request of the base commander, Col. William H. Blanchard. Blanchard, according to Mr. Haut, was very interested in maintaining good relations between the base and the Roswell community. "If anything unusual happened, or anything he felt the community should know about, he would call me and say, 'Get this thing out.' He did that with many, many things."

There is no doubt in Mr. Haut's mind that Blanchard and Marcel were convinced the debris found by the rancher came from another planet. There is also no doubt in Mr. Haut's mind today that Blanchard did not originate the idea of contacting the press:

"Do you think somebody was ordering Blanchard to order you to issue the press release?"

"Yes, I do," said Mr. Haut in a telephone interview on January 28, 1994. He took the press release to the radio station KGFL and the Roswell Morning Dispatch, which in turn communicated the story to the wire services. Within an hour, telephone lines into Roswell and the base were jammed with calls from all over the world.

Art McQuiddy, then editor of the Roswell *Morning Dispatch*, reports that the reaction was almost immediate.

"By the time Haut had gotten to me it hadn't been 10 minutes and the phones starting ringing. I didn't get off the phone until late that afternoon. I had calls from London and Paris and Rome and Hong Kong that I can remember," he said.

Within hours, an official retraction was released by the government. Jesse Marcel was brought in to prop up the official "cover story" that what was found was a weather balloon. Marcel, in his later years, however, was very willing to admit that he was ordered by military superiors to make untrue statements.

The Roswell base was then key in the nuclear bomb strategy of the U.S. government. The Cold War was just starting, and World War II had just ended. In those days, when Uncle Sam said shut up few people asked why. This was particularly the case in New Mexico, where such sensitive military installations as Los Alamos and White Sands were located.

The next morning at 6 o'clock, the sheriff went to Glenn's parents' home and spoke to his father, saying that Glenn "might" be in trouble. Glenn's parents related that the Chavez County sheriff reported that the military had interviewed him. They became worried their son was in trouble.

The Roswell *Daily Record* of Tuesday, July 8, and Wednesday, July 9, 1947, spans the course of the initial press flurry turning to a cover story. "RAAF Captures Flying Saucer on Ranch in Roswell Region," trumpeted the Tuesday headline. The story stated that Marcel's recovery of a disc retrieved "on a ranch in the Roswell vicinity, after an unidentified rancher had notified Sheriff Geo. Wilcox, here, that he had found the instrument on his premises."

Mr. and Mrs. Dan Wilmmot of Roswell are also included in the same story, recounting their sighting of an oval object that was about 15 to 20 feet in diameter and about five feet thick, traveling at 400 to 500 miles per hour in a northwesterly direction. "In appearance it looked oval in shape like two inverted saucers faced mouth to mouth, or like two old type washbowls placed together in the same fashion. The entire body glowed as though light were showing through from inside, though not like it would be if a light were merely underneath," they said.

Roswellians were surveyed by the paper as to their

opinions of the story and most thought it was some sort of secret government craft. The next issue of the *Daily Record* gives insight into the excitement stirred up worldwide by Tuesday's story. Sheriff Wilcox is photographed talking on the phone to "a high English official." However, the story describes the incident as "the world comedy, which developed over the purported finding of a flying saucer."

The numerous calls from reporters around the world are mentioned. Wednesday's headline sets the overall tone: "Gen. Ramey Empties Roswell Saucer." Brig. Gen. Roger M. Ramey, head of the Eighth Air Force, called the remains a weather balloon, the paper reported.

Weather experts were quoted to the effect that this was the most likely explanation. A bizarrely written UFO sighting from Iran is placed above Ramey's explanation as if to ridicule the flying saucer story. The rancher who found the object, W.W. "Mac" Brazel, is quoted saying, "If I find anything else besides a bomb they are going to have a hard time getting me to say anything about it."

The object is described throughout the article as "a balloon." This, on the surface of it, seemed to put the matter to rest. It is interesting to note a tiny item just above the Brazel story, which mentions a meeting between U.S. Senator Carl A. Hatch, of New Mexico, and President Truman on July 9. While it was described as being "just a personal visit," a former employee of the Roswell radio station who interviewed Mac Brazel said that the station owner received a call from the office of New Mexico's other U.S. Senator, Dennis Chavez, warning him not to broadcast the interview if he wanted his license renewed.

It is now known that Lt. Gen. Nathan F. Twining, the commander of Air Material Command, headquartered at Wright Field in Ohio, made a sudden visit to Alamogordo Army Air Field in New Mexico on July 7, 1947. This was a short drive from Roswell. On the next day, Glenn Dennis received his mysterious phone calls and made his visit to the base.

Twining, later on, became the head of the Joint Chiefs of Staff. Neither Mr. Haut nor Co. Blanchard suffered any career repercussions. Mr. Haut, prior to the incident, had already decided to retire from the military and settle in Roswell, which he did in 1948. Col. Blanchard went on to become a general. Marcel went on to do research on the Soviet nuclear program. When President Truman announced that the Soviet Union had exploded a nuclear bomb, the report he read to the public was written by Jesse Marcel.

As to where the bodies of the aliens are today, Stanton Friedman says: "It is anybody's guess." The nurse who spoke with Glenn in the Officer's Club said she believed the bodies ended up in Ohio. Numerous rumors have circulated for years concerning the alleged presence of alien bodies at Wright Patterson Air Force Base near Dayton, Ohio. Stanton Friedman believes the bodies may have been studied for a time at a private clinic in Albuquerque, N.M.

It was also reported that the Fort Worth, Texas, headquarters of the Eighth Air Force and Gen. Ramey, was the first destination of the crate containing the bodies after it left Roswell. The bombardier of the plane that transported the crate reported the flight was met in

Fort Worth by, among others, a man the bombardier personally knew to be a mortician. The identity of this mortician is unknown.

However, the identity of the other mortician who played a role in this event is well-known. Glenn Dennis has neither sought notoriety nor tried to hide from researchers. He has an interesting story to tell, as do others involved in the same event now willing to talk about it in their sunset years.

Would arterial embalming work on an extraterrestrial? Embalming fluid uses formalin, which changes the chemical composition of protein by acting on nitrogen. All life forms on earth are protein-based organisms. If alien bodies were recovered, and if they were protein-based organisms, then preservation could have been achieved.

No funeral was held for the remains of these stranded travelers. However, the book *The Roswell Incident* by Charles Berlitz and William L. Moore, contains an account of the government's providing a private viewing for a member of the clergy. This book includes a letter allegedly written on April 19, 1954, which describes a February 20, 1954, visit to Edwards Air Force Base in California by President Eisenhower to view the bodies of alien pilots of a crashed UFO. Bishop (later Cardinal)

James F.A. McIntyre of Los Angeles, Edward Nourse of the Brookings Institute, and journalist Franklin Allen were also permitted to view the bodies. The letter goes on to say that Eisenhower was about to "go directly to the people via radio and television" to spill the beans on UFOs. Evidently, he changed his mind, or else the letter is a fraud.

It should be mentioned that there is a point of controversy within the community of UFO researchers as to whether there was two or just one UFO crash in New Mexico in July 1947. Stanton Friedman believes that another UFO (with more alien bodies) was recovered on the plains of San Agustin—about 150 miles to the west of Roswell, New Mexico. It is thought that these two vehicles may have collided. Other UFO researchers—specifically Donald Schmidt—believe that the Roswell crash was the only such incident to occur in New Mexico at that time.

Some also believe that after the Roswell crash, a supersecret government group called Majestic 12 was established to oversee all UFO-related events. Mr. Friedman has done extensive research into the subject, the results of which are found in his book *Crash at Corona*. He has studied documents allegedly generated by this secret group and believes them genuine.

A made-for-TV movie, *Roswell*, was broadcast last July. Mr. Haut was an advisor for the movie.

Thanks to Glenn Dennis, Walter Haut, and the UFO Museum in Roswell, N.M.; Stanton Friedman, Fredericton, New Brunswick, Canada; Richard Heiden, Milwaukee; Richard Nelson, Mid-America College of Mortuary Science; Prof. John Salter,University of North Dakota at Grand Forks; and Gary Sime,Readstown, Wis.

BIBLIOGRAPHY

Berlitz, Charles, and Moore, William L., "The Roswell Incident," Berkley Books, New York, 1988.

Friedman, Stanton, and Berliner, Don, "Crash at Corona," Paragon House, New York.

Schmidt, Donald, and Randle, Kevin, "UFO Crash at Roswell," Avon Books, New York, 1992

THE PRECEDING ARTICLE PUBLISHED IN THE NOVEMBER 1994 ISSUE OF *AMERICAN FUNERAL DIRECTOR* COPYRIGHT AMERICAN FUNERAL DIRECTOR 1994, KATES-BOYLSTON PUBLICATIONS, INC. 1501 BROADWAY, NEW YORK, N.Y. 10036 REPRINTED WITH PERMISSION OF THE EDITORS

ABOUT ATMOSPHERE PRESS

Atmosphere Press is an independent, full-service publisher for excellent books in all genres and for all audiences. Learn more about what we do at atmosphere-press.com.

We encourage you to check out some of Atmosphere's latest releases, which are available at Amazon.com and via order from your local bookstore:

The Embers of Tradition, a novel by Chukwudum Okeke

Saints and Martyrs: A Novel, by Aaron Roe

When I Am Ashes, a novel by Amber Rose

Melancholy Vision: A Revolution Series Novel, by L.C. Hamilton

The Recoleta Stories, by Bryon Esmond Butler

Voodoo Hideaway, a novel by Vance Cariaga

Hart Street and Main, a novel by Tabitha Sprunger

The Weed Lady, a novel by Shea R. Embry

A Book of Life, a novel by David Ellis

ABOUT THE AUTHOR

Photo credit: Max Firebaugh

John H. Sime was born in 1952 in Viroqua, Wisconsin. He studied Comparative Literature (BA74, MA76) at the University of Wisconsin-Madison. He served in the US Peace Corps in Mali. He studied at the Kentucky School of Mortuary Science in Louisville. He worked in the funeral profession for more than forty years. In the 1990s he was a Sysop on the CompuServe UFO Forum. He has published poetry, fiction, and non fiction in *Kickapoo Free Press, Poetry Wisconsin, Howling Mantra, Contours,* and *American Funeral Director.* He is the author of two novels, *No Place to Go* and *Rabblerouser,* and two collections of poetry, *A River Called Kickapoo* and *Ain't No Elephants in Timbuktu.*

<u>UFO, a haiku</u>

They are out there now.
Other worlds await and watch.
Don't go back to sleep.

(posted on CompuServe UFO forum
when Whitley Strieber was a monthly guest.
He responded: "keep on rocking.")